D1328251

EYEWITNESS BOOKS

TREE

Blue atlas cedar

Rowan berries and leaves

White pine cone

Acorns

Magnolia leaf

Apples

Monterey cypress

Willow

Hazelnuts

Victoria plum fruit

Ginkgo leaf

Sycamore seeds

EYEWITNESS BOOKS

Ornamental apple fruit

TREE

Written by
DAVID BURNIE

Lodgepole
pine cones

Ash leaf

Fungus feeding
on decaying
wood

Oak wood

Hazelnuts

Moss on
decaying wood

Stoddart

Lawson cypress cones

Sequoia cone

Pine cone

Western
red cedar leaves

Pear

Japanese
maple leaf

Larch cones

Rowan leaf

Series editor Janice Lacock
Art editor Carole Ash
Special photography
Peter Chadwick, Philip Dowell,
and Kim Taylor
Editorial consultants
The staff of the Natural History Museum, London

First published in 1988 by
STODDART PUBLISHING CO. LIMITED
34 Lesmill Road
Toronto, Canada
M3B 2T6
This edition reprinted in 1988

First published in the United Kingdom by
Dorling Kindersley

Copyright © 1988 Dorling Kindersley Limited, London
and Editions Gallimard, Paris
Text copyright © 1988 Dorling Kindersley Limited, London
Illustration copyright © 1988 Dorling Kindersley Limited, London

All rights reserved. No part of this publication
may be reproduced, stored in a retrieval system,
or transmitted in any form or by any means, electronic,
mechanical, photocopying, recording or otherwise, without
the prior written permission of the copyright owner.

Canadian Cataloguing in Publication Data
Main entry under title:
Tree
(Eye witness series)
Includes index
ISBN 0-7737-2181-9

1. Trees - Juvenile literature. I. Series.

QK475.8.T73 1988   j582.16   C88-093215-5

Young Scotch
pine cones

Color reproduction by Colourscan, Singapore
Typeset by Windsor Graphics, Ringwood, Hampshire
Printed in Italy by A. Mondadori Editore, Verona

Vine-leaved
maple leaf

Variegated
holly leaf

Osier leaf

Contents

Yew leaves

Ginkgo leaf

Hemlock cones

What is a tree?

THE EARLIEST "PLANTS" were so small that it would have taken dozens of them to cover a pinhead. These tiny cells lived in the oceans of the ancient Earth, and the only thing that enables us to classify them as plants was that they could use sunlight to grow. From these humble beginnings, the whole plant kingdom as we know it today has evolved. Many plants remained in water, but others began to grow on land. To do this successfully, they needed a way to support themselves. Some plants eventually developed a material called lignin, which made their stems tough and woody so that they could grow taller. Because all plants need light, the tall plants did better than the small ones, which had to survive in their shade. In time, plants with a giant single stem appeared: these were the first trees. Since then trees have evolved many times, in different families of plants. The bulkiest - the giant sequoias of California - can weigh more than 6,000 tons, making them the heaviest living things ever to have existed on Earth.

HOMAGE IN STONE
This tree goddess was carved on a Hindu shrine in India, c. 150 A.D.

Spreading base connects tree to a circle of roots (pp. 18-19) that anchors it in ground

Rugged, cracked bark (pp. 22-23) at base of tree

Broken branch may allow fungi to penetrate trunk

Trunks (pp. 20-21) are longest and straightest in trees grown close together

The tree in mythology

All over the world, from the dark forests of Scandinavia to the banyan groves of India, trees have figured in ancient myths, folklore, and rituals. Perhaps because of the size and long life of trees, many religions have regarded them as sacred symbols, and certain individual trees have been worshiped as gods. Hindus, for example, revere the banyan tree; the Druids worshiped the oak.

CHRISTIAN BELIEF
In the Bible, the cross on which Christ died was symbolically linked with the tree of life, which grew in the garden of Eden along with the tree of knowledge and offered everlasting life.

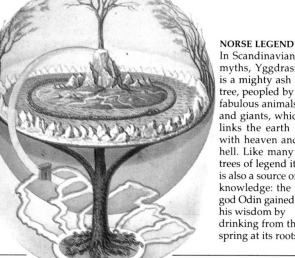

NORSE LEGEND
In Scandinavian myths, Yggdrasil is a mighty ash tree, peopled by fabulous animals and giants, which links the earth with heaven and hell. Like many trees of legend it is also a source of knowledge: the god Odin gained his wisdom by drinking from the spring at its roots.

TREE OR NOT?
A tree is a tall plant with a single woody stem. The three main groups of trees are the broadleaves (pp. 8-9), the conifers (pp. 10-11), and the palms (pp. 12-13). There are several other treelike plants, including tree ferns, cycads, and giant bamboo (shown here).

Bark becomes smoother higher up the tree

Each spring, twigs, leaves, and flowers (pp. 32-37) develop from buds (pp. 24-25)

Branches stay at same height above ground as tree grows, becoming thicker each year

DAPHNE TRANSFORMED
Greek legend has it that to escape from the amorous Apollo, the goddess Daphne changed into a laurel tree. Today the laurel has a symbolic use as a token of victory, just as it did in ancient Greece.

In summer, deciduous trees have a dense canopy of leaves (pp. 26-31)

Broadleaved trees

Hedge maple

Five thousand years ago, before the spread of agriculture, huge areas of Europe and eastern North America were cloaked in broadleaved forest. Since then much of the forest has been cleared to make way for people. Despite this, woodlands with stately broadleaved trees such as oaks, beeches, and maples still remain in many places and make up an extremely important natural habitat. Broadleaved trees are so named because most of them have broad, flat leaves, quite unlike the needles and scales of conifers. They all produce flowers, and after pollination (pp. 32-37) these flowers develop seeds. The seeds are often enclosed in a hard nut or a fleshy fruit. Many broadleaved trees shed their leaves every autumn: that is, they are deciduous (p. 46).

Young acorns attached to long stalks

BROADLEAVED WOODLAND
Natural woodlands are powerhouses of biological activity. The trees' leaves intercept sunlight and use it to provide the energy they need to grow (p. 16). Every year they produce huge quantities of wood, leaves, flowers, fruit, and seeds. These make up the food of millions of woodland animals that range from tiny invertebrates (animals without backbones), such as micromoths (p. 51), to large mammals, such as deer.

Oak in winter

Oak in full summer foliage

THE WINTER SLEEP
Broadleaved trees are most common in warm climates. To survive in colder regions, they have evolved a form of "hibernation" in which they shed their leaves and become dormant (inactive) until spring.

Lichen growing on bark

THE OAKS
Oaks are typical broadleaved trees. About 600 species are found around the world. Some oaks, like the English oak shown here, are deciduous; others are evergreen. All oaks are wind pollinated (p. 32), and all produce acorns. Oak wood is exceptionally hard and durable.

Young acorns on long stalks

Narrow growth rings

Hard wood, resistant to decay

Leaf litter, rich in rotting fungi and invertebrate animals

Crooked branches grow at irregular intervals

SHAPED BY THE ENVIRONMENT
A tree's position can affect its shape. In windswept places, twigs and branches on the side facing the wind are killed, so a tree becomes lopsided. A tree growing close to others grows mainly upward as it reaches for light; a tree in the open forms a leafy, spreading crown.

Irregular shape caused by strong winds

A beech growing in an open site

Beeches growing on a plantation

BROADLEAVED GROWTH PATTERNS
Broadleaved trees like oaks generally have a spreading growth pattern. In most species the trunk divides into many spreading branches of similar size. This is quite unlike the more upward growth of conifers (p. 10).

Broad, leathery leaves in clusters at tips of shoots

Coniferous trees

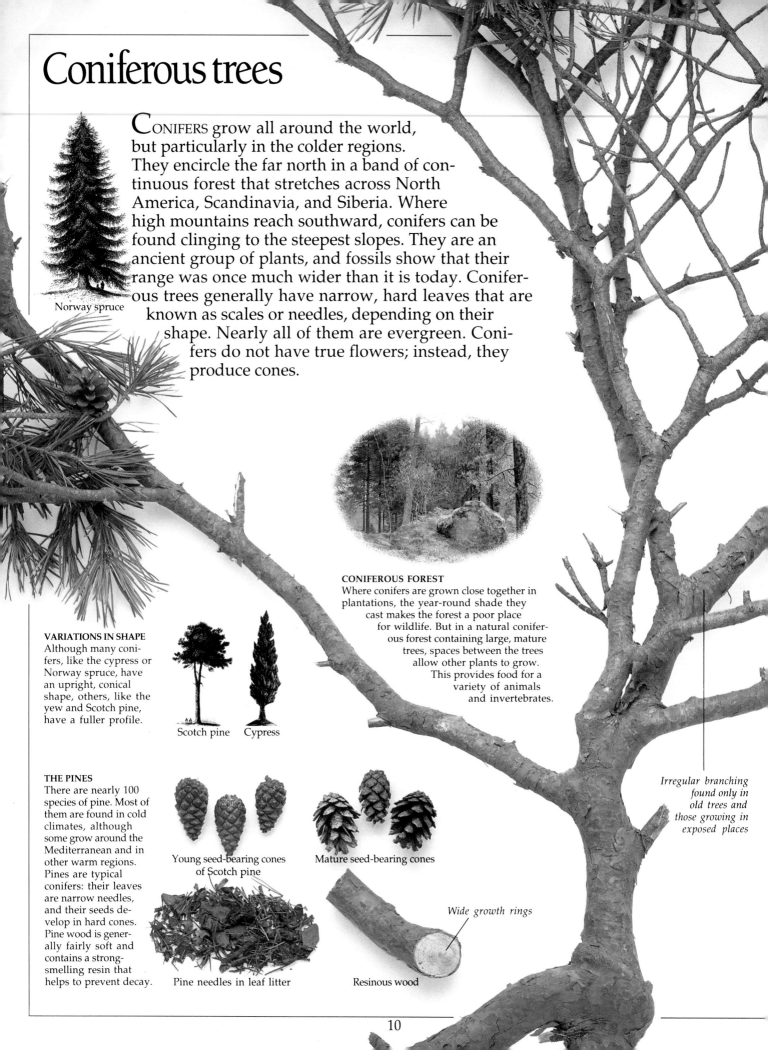

CONIFERS grow all around the world, but particularly in the colder regions. They encircle the far north in a band of continuous forest that stretches across North America, Scandinavia, and Siberia. Where high mountains reach southward, conifers can be found clinging to the steepest slopes. They are an ancient group of plants, and fossils show that their range was once much wider than it is today. Coniferous trees generally have narrow, hard leaves that are known as scales or needles, depending on their shape. Nearly all of them are evergreen. Conifers do not have true flowers; instead, they produce cones.

Norway spruce

CONIFEROUS FOREST
Where conifers are grown close together in plantations, the year-round shade they cast makes the forest a poor place for wildlife. But in a natural coniferous forest containing large, mature trees, spaces between the trees allow other plants to grow. This provides food for a variety of animals and invertebrates.

VARIATIONS IN SHAPE
Although many conifers, like the cypress or Norway spruce, have an upright, conical shape, others, like the yew and Scotch pine, have a fuller profile.

Scotch pine   Cypress

Irregular branching found only in old trees and those growing in exposed places

THE PINES
There are nearly 100 species of pine. Most of them are found in cold climates, although some grow around the Mediterranean and in other warm regions. Pines are typical conifers: their leaves are narrow needles, and their seeds develop in hard cones. Pine wood is generally fairly soft and contains a strong-smelling resin that helps to prevent decay.

Young seed-bearing cones of Scotch pine

Mature seed-bearing cones

Wide growth rings

Pine needles in leaf litter

Resinous wood

Bark at the top of a mature Scotch pine flakes off in thin, reddish patches

New female cones take almost two years to ripen and shed their seeds.

Hard blue-green needles carried in pairs around the sides of the shoots

CHRISTMAS CONIFERS
Although trees have been used as ornaments for hundreds of years at Christmas, the custom of decorating Norway spruces and other conifers became really widespread in the 19th century. Evergreen decorations, however, were used long before the arrival of Christianity: in pagan midwinter festivals the green foliage of holly or conifers signaled the return of spring.

CONIFER GROWTH PATTERN
In most young conifers there is a strong leading shoot, and short side branches are thrown out at regular intervals. Later in life their growth may become much less symmetrical (even), as the gnarled and twisted branches of this Scotch pine show.

Tropical trees

Palm

ALTHOUGH TROPICAL TREES do not have to face harsh winters, their growth is affected by another factor - rain. In some parts of the tropics, rain falls all year round. In these hothouse conditions, broadleaved trees can grow at an extraordinary rate - 15 ft (5 m) a year is quite common for some saplings. So crowded are the trees that, area for area, tropical rain forest supports the biggest weight of living matter of any land habitat on Earth. Where there is less rain, trees struggle more against drought than against each other. In places with wet and dry seasons, many trees shed their leaves to survive the water shortage. Trees like palms and eucalyptuses, which often live in places that are very dry, often have tough, leathery leaves to keep hot winds from drying them out.

BENEATH THE CANOPY
In tropical rain forest, the unbroken "canopy" formed by the treetops casts a deep shade on the forest floor.

BUTTRESS ROOTS
In tropical rain forests, trees often grow to great heights to compete with their neighbors for sunlight. Where the soil is thin, the trees are in danger of toppling over, so some species have evolved buttress roots that spread out and stabilize their trunks.

NATURAL DRAINAGE
Many tropical trees have leaves with pointed tips. These work like gargoyles on old buildings, throwing off the water in heavy downpours. The tree shown here is a weeping fig, which is found in India and southeast Asia.

Drip tip throws off rainwater

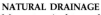

RECORD-BREAKING EUCALYPTUSES
Eucalyptuses are some of the fastest-growing trees in the world. They are mainly found in the parched outback and subtropical forests of Australia; some species also grow near the snow line on the continent's mountains.

Tree fern

ISLAND JUNGLE
This dense tangle of vegetation is typical of the rain forest of northern Australia. Cooler forests in Australia and New Zealand are the home of many species of tree ferns, plants that look like palms but are quite unrelated to them.

Leaves unfold like fans as they grow

Eucalyptus leaves contain oil and attract koala bears (p. 51)

THE ONE-TREE FOREST
The banyan is an extraordinary tropical tree that spreads by forming pillar roots. These develop from roots that grow down from the banyan's branches. One banyan in Calcutta has over a thousand pillar roots, giving it the largest spread of any tree on Earth.

Single, fibrous unbranched stem

THE PALMS
There are just under 3,000 species of palms in the world, nearly all of them found only in the tropics. The coconut palm's nuts float on seawater until they are thrown up on land. The liquid or "milk" in the nut allows the seed to germinate on dry beaches.

Each nut is surrounded by a waterproof, lightweight husk

Roots emerge through husk

13

The birth of a tree

Mature beech tree, over 150 years old, growing in parkland

FOR ANY TREE, the first few months of life are far more hazardous than the decades, or even centuries, that follow them. While it is true that "tall oaks from little acorns grow," only a tiny fraction of a tree's seeds actually survive that long. In a good year a single oak tree will produce about 50,000 acorns. But most of these will be eaten by animals or fall to places where they cannot grow. Those that do develop into seedlings run the risk of being eaten or trampled on by animals. Only a handful will still be alive a year later. All seeds have a store of food that provides energy to keep them alive and to fuel germination and growth. In some seeds, like those of willows, this store is so tiny that the seeds must germinate within days of being shed. On the other hand, the seeds of trees like the oak and beech contain enough food to stay alive for a whole winter. Germination - the real birth of the tree - begins as soon as the days grow warmer in the spring.

5 SHEDDING THE SEEDCASE
Fourteen days after germination the two seed leaves, or cotyledons, expand. These were previously folded inside the seed, but now they force the seedcase off, and it drops to the ground. Until this moment, the seed has relied entirely on its internal food reserves - now its seed leaves will start to provide it with energy.

Seedcase forced off by seed leaves

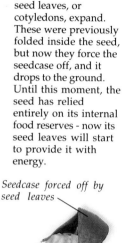

Emerging seed leaves

4 GROWING UP
Five days after germination, the seed-case has been lifted off the ground by the developing stem. As the root grows deeper into the ground, rootlets start to branch out just below soil level.

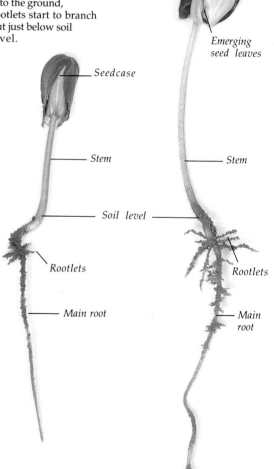

Seedcase

Stem

Stem

Soil level

Rootlets

Rootlets

Main root

Main root

Seedcase curling back

Three-sided seed attached to case

Crack caused by swelling embryo

Seedcase

Seedcase

Emerging root

1 THE FALL TO EARTH
The beech tree produces its seeds, also called beech mast or beechnuts, in woody cases. The tree grows a heavy crop in "mast years," which occur about one year in three. Some seeds drop when the woody cases open while still attached to the tree, and others fall to the ground while still attached to the case.

2 GERMINATION BEGINS
During the winter months many of the seeds that lie scattered under a beech tree are eaten by hungry squirrels, wood mice, finches, and jays. Those seeds that are lucky enough to survive begin to germinate in early spring. The first sign of life is a crack in the seed's hard shell as the embryo inside it begins to expand.

3 GETTING A GRIP
The developing embryo needs a firm foothold in the ground. A root appears from the pointed end of the seed and grows directly downward. It collects water and minerals from the soil and anchors the seed.

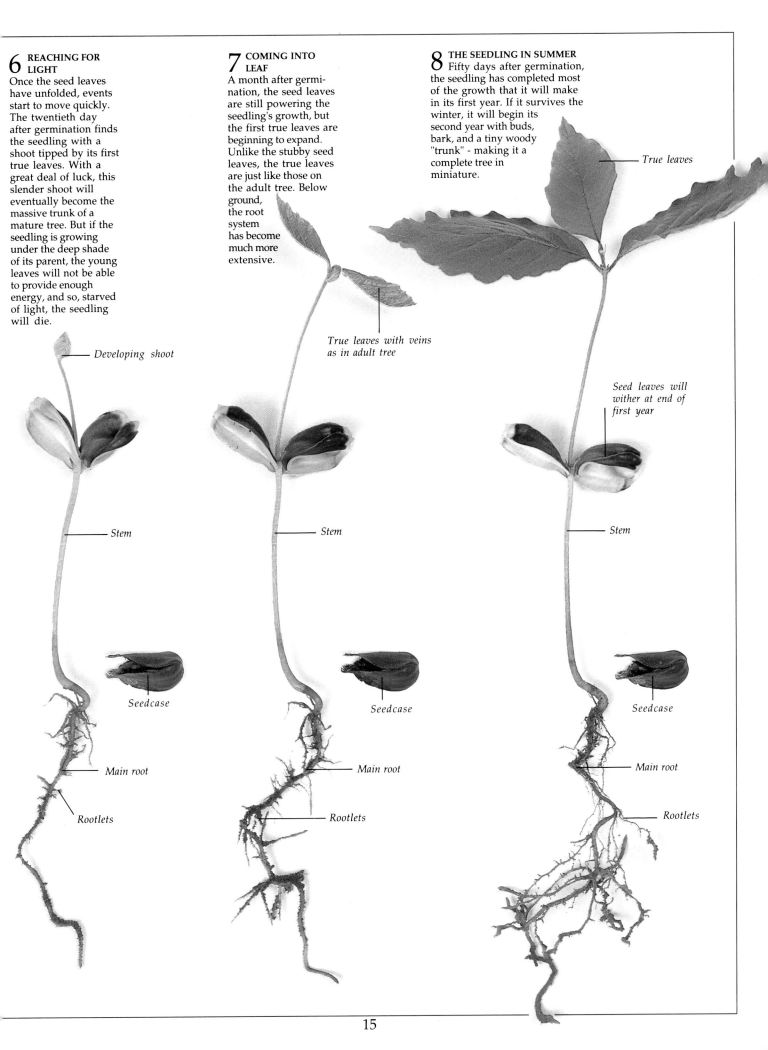

6 REACHING FOR LIGHT

Once the seed leaves have unfolded, events start to move quickly. The twentieth day after germination finds the seedling with a shoot tipped by its first true leaves. With a great deal of luck, this slender shoot will eventually become the massive trunk of a mature tree. But if the seedling is growing under the deep shade of its parent, the young leaves will not be able to provide enough energy, and so, starved of light, the seedling will die.

Developing shoot

Stem

Seedcase

Main root

Rootlets

7 COMING INTO LEAF

A month after germination, the seed leaves are still powering the seedling's growth, but the first true leaves are beginning to expand. Unlike the stubby seed leaves, the true leaves are just like those on the adult tree. Below ground, the root system has become much more extensive.

True leaves with veins as in adult tree

Stem

Seedcase

Main root

Rootlets

8 THE SEEDLING IN SUMMER

Fifty days after germination, the seedling has completed most of the growth that it will make in its first year. If it survives the winter, it will begin its second year with buds, bark, and a tiny woody "trunk" - making it a complete tree in miniature.

True leaves

Seed leaves will wither at end of first year

Stem

Seedcase

Main root

Rootlets

15

How trees grow

A LIVING SKIN
Despite losing its heartwood inside, this ash tree survives. It is the outer layer of sapwood that carries water and sap.

Trees grow in two different ways. At the tip of every twig there is a group of specialized cells. When these cells divide they make the twig grow longer, and so the tree grows taller or spreads more. At the same time, a different kind of growth is produced by the cambium, a layer of cells that covers the woody part of the tree. As the cells in the cambium divide, the trunk, branches, twigs, and roots grow fatter. The girth of, or distance around, most mature tree trunks increases by roughly 1 in (2.5 cm) every year. In temperate climates, both kinds of growth usually occur in the spring and summer only. The cambium grows outward and the new cells that it produces form a visible ring - one for each year. By counting these rings, it is possible to figure out the age of the tree.

HIDDEN STRENGTH
As trees grow, the force produced by their expanding roots is tremendous. This tree in Cambodia is gradually breaking up the old temple wall on which it grows.

THE HEAVIEST TREES
Sequoias and California redwoods grow on mountainsides watered by fog that rolls in from the Pacific Ocean. Because there are few strong winds, the trees' growth is not stopped, and they often reach exceptional heights.

Heartwood - composed mostly of dead cells

Sapwood - composed of living cells

Bark

Sapwood - composed of living cells

SLOW GROWTH
This branch from a yew tree is over 75 years old. Its growth rings are packed closely together.

FAST GROWTH
This branch from a sycamore tree is only about 15 years old. Its growth rings are widely spaced.

GROUND HUGGERS
In the Arctic tundra, conditions are too severe for trees to grow. Instead, flattened shrubs, like this dwarf willow, flourish.

Area of rapid growth

Area of slow growth

Sap stain in partially seasoned wood

THE OLDEST TREES
Bristlecone pines are among the oldest living things on Earth. These pines grow in the Rocky Mountains; at high altitudes their growth is extremely slow. Some specimens are estimated to be 6,000 years old.

Bark

LOPSIDED GROWTH
As trees grow, their trunks and branches do not always expand at the same rate all the way around. Off-center growth rings like these can be produced in two different ways. If a tree grows in an exposed place, its wood grows faster on the side facing away from the wind than it does on the windward side. With large branches, faster growth often occurs on the underside to help support the weight of the branch.

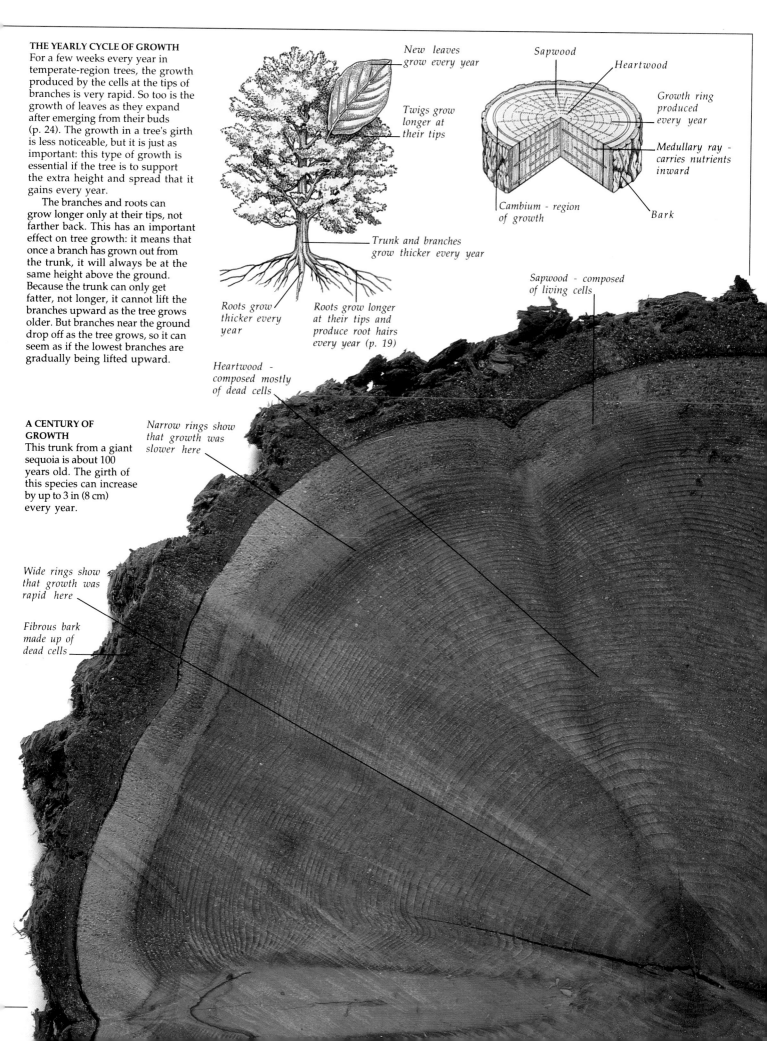

THE YEARLY CYCLE OF GROWTH

For a few weeks every year in temperate-region trees, the growth produced by the cells at the tips of branches is very rapid. So too is the growth of leaves as they expand after emerging from their buds (p. 24). The growth in a tree's girth is less noticeable, but it is just as important: this type of growth is essential if the tree is to support the extra height and spread that it gains every year.

The branches and roots can grow longer only at their tips, not farther back. This has an important effect on tree growth: it means that once a branch has grown out from the trunk, it will always be at the same height above the ground. Because the trunk can only get fatter, not longer, it cannot lift the branches upward as the tree grows older. But branches near the ground drop off as the tree grows, so it can seem as if the lowest branches are gradually being lifted upward.

New leaves grow every year

Twigs grow longer at their tips

Trunk and branches grow thicker every year

Roots grow thicker every year

Roots grow longer at their tips and produce root hairs every year (p. 19)

Sapwood

Heartwood

Growth ring produced every year

Medullary ray - carries nutrients inward

Cambium - region of growth

Bark

Sapwood - composed of living cells

Heartwood - composed mostly of dead cells

A CENTURY OF GROWTH

This trunk from a giant sequoia is about 100 years old. The girth of this species can increase by up to 3 in (8 cm) every year.

Narrow rings show that growth was slower here

Wide rings show that growth was rapid here

Fibrous bark made up of dead cells

Putting down roots

Badgers pass their tunnels on from generation to generation. As a tree grows, a badger "set" grows with it, as the animals harmlessly dig new tunnels among the spreading roots

Bᴇᴄᴀᴜsᴇ ᴛʀᴇᴇs ᴀʀᴇ ᴛʜᴇ ᴛᴀʟʟᴇsᴛ ʟɪᴠɪɴɢ ᴘʟᴀɴᴛs, it is easy to think that their roots plunge down deep into the earth. But this is often far from the truth. Instead of growing downward, most of a tree's roots grow outward, forming a crisscrossing net that anchors the tree in the ground.

The roots of a tree 165 ft (50 m) tall are likely to reach no more than 8 ft (2.5 m) into the ground, but they may well spread outward to a distance that matches the tree's height. This means that the roots of a 165-foot tree cover an area the size of a very large football field. Over all this ground, tiny root hairs collect water and minerals and channel them into rootlets. The precious water passes from the rootlets into the main roots and finally, after a long journey, into the trunk.

Roots for waterlogged ground

Most trees are unable to grow in ground that is permanently waterlogged because the soil is unstable and moves around. It is also very low in oxygen, which tree roots need. A few trees can live in these conditions. Mangroves are tropical trees that grow on coastal mud flats. They have two special kinds of roots: stilt-roots arch from the mangrove's trunk and anchor the tree in mud; breathing roots, or pneumatophores, grow up through the mud and are exposed to the air at low tide, enabling them to collect oxygen. The bald cypress is another tree that has breathing roots. This unusual conifer lives in the freshwater swamps of the southern United States, where there is little oxygen in the still water.

MANGROVE SWAMP
Mangroves face little competition from other plants. On some tropical coasts they form bands of vegetation hundreds of miles long.

COMING UP FOR AIR
The bald cypress flourishes in the bayou country of the southern United States. It has two unusual characteristics - its knobbly breathing roots, and the fact that it is a deciduous conifer.

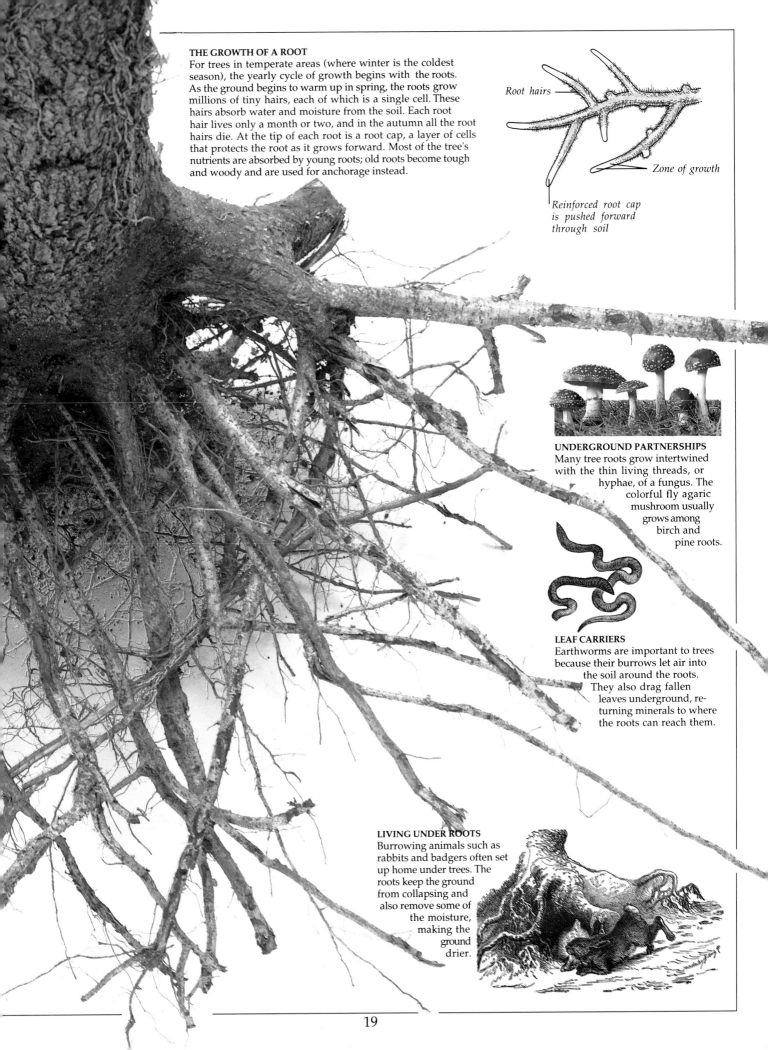

THE GROWTH OF A ROOT

For trees in temperate areas (where winter is the coldest season), the yearly cycle of growth begins with the roots. As the ground begins to warm up in spring, the roots grow millions of tiny hairs, each of which is a single cell. These hairs absorb water and moisture from the soil. Each root hair lives only a month or two, and in the autumn all the root hairs die. At the tip of each root is a root cap, a layer of cells that protects the root as it grows forward. Most of the tree's nutrients are absorbed by young roots; old roots become tough and woody and are used for anchorage instead.

Root hairs

Zone of growth

Reinforced root cap
is pushed forward
through soil

UNDERGROUND PARTNERSHIPS

Many tree roots grow intertwined with the thin living threads, or hyphae, of a fungus. The colorful fly agaric mushroom usually grows among birch and pine roots.

LEAF CARRIERS

Earthworms are important to trees because their burrows let air into the soil around the roots. They also drag fallen leaves underground, returning minerals to where the roots can reach them.

LIVING UNDER ROOTS

Burrowing animals such as rabbits and badgers often set up home under trees. The roots keep the ground from collapsing and also remove some of the moisture, making the ground drier.

The tree trunk

Just below the surface of a tree's trunk, constant but invisible flows of sap draw minerals up from the ground and carry nutrients downward from the leaves (p. 17). The tree guards this rich pathway for food with its covering of tough bark. Even so, insects, fungi, and parasitic plants sometimes manage to break through this barrier and reach what lies beneath. Nourished by the food that they have plundered from the tree, these animals form the base of the tree-trunk food chain. Fungi rot the wood and open it to other attackers, while the larvae of countless insects, from beetles to wood wasps, make up the food of woodland birds.

THE SPIRAL CREEPER
Tree creepers are small mouse-colored birds that feed on tree-trunk insects. They are unique in the way they climb each trunk by spiraling around it.

THE LIVING LARDER
Many mammals, such as squirrels, take away tree seeds and bury them. But they do not find later all the seeds they have stored, and many of these seeds survive to germinate. The acorn woodpecker of south-western America stores acorns in an obvious place - in trees or telegraph poles. It bores holes and pushes an acorn into each one. It may cover a single tree with hundreds of holes.

Acorns in pine bark

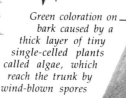

Acorn woodpecker on a tree trunk

Hole in dead wood dug by a woodpecker and used for nesting; the surrounding bark has healed after a small branch dropped away

Green coloration on bark caused by a thick layer of tiny single-celled plants called algae, which reach the trunk by wind-blown spores

Living bark growing over dead heartwood

Fruiting bodies of fungus - it has infected damp wood

LIFE ON THE TRUNK
This trunk is from a mature Norway maple. Fungi and insects will attack where dead wood is exposed, but the tree will survive as long as enough living wood is left to supply water to the leaves.

"Eye" in bark - the scar left by a young branch that was shed

Nuthatch and young

Cross section of nuthatch nest

TREE-TRUNK ACROBATS
Although most large birds cannot support their weight while clinging to a vertical tree trunk, smaller species have no difficulty doing so. Their agility enables them to collect rich pickings in the form of insects that live in bark crevices. Many of these birds fly from tree to tree, working their way upward as they quickly scan the trunk for food. The nuthatch is alone among them in being able to walk down a trunk as well as up it.

Bark damaged by squirrels in search of the tree's sugar-rich sap

Healthy side branch with complete bark covering

IMPRISONED INSIDE A TREE
Some birds that nest in tree-trunk holes adapt the entrance size and shape by adding mud to it. This habit is taken to extremes by tree hornbills. The female seals the nest entrance with a mixture of mud and saliva, leaving just a small hole so that her mate can feed her. The mud entrance dries to become very hard, preventing predators from breaking in to attack the mother and fledglings. While she is trapped inside her cell, the female bird molts, and may be almost bald for some weeks.

Side galleries dug by growing larvae

Eggs laid at intervals along main gallery

Main gallery dug by mother beetle

Bark beetle galleries

Bark beetles

Pine weevil

INSECT MINERS
The young of bark beetles dig galleries as they eat their way through the wood.

WOOD BORERS
Adult weevils can spread disease and damage shoots by using their long snouts to chew at the bark.

PASSENGERS AND PARASITES
Trees often play host to smaller plants, most of which do no harm to them. Mosses, lichens, and ferns are common on trees in temperate regions; in the tropics they are joined by much flashier plants such as orchids and bromeliads. More threatening is the mistletoe: its sticky seed, which is scraped off a bird's beak onto the host tree's bark, produces a root that grows into the living wood. The parasitic mistletoe then extracts nutritious sap from the tree. Because most of its food comes from the tree, the mistletoe has little need of its leaves, which are small and leathery to the touch.

Bark- the outer skin

Bark from an ash sapling

A TREE'S BARK IS ITS SKIN. It protects the tree from attack by animals and fungi, from drying out, and even, in eucalyptuses and redwoods, from being damaged by forest fires. Just like skin, bark is made up of two layers. The inner layer, called the bark cambium, consists of living cells that are constantly dividing. Produced in their millions, these cells die when they are cut off from the supply of water and sap. But when dead they become the outer bark and form a highly effective barrier against the elements.

RUBBER TAPPING
Most of the world's rubber is made from white latex collected from cuts made in the bark of certain trees originally found in the Amazon basin in South America.

THICK AND THIN SKINS
Bark varies enormously in thickness. The bark of redwoods, like that of the sequoia on the opposite page, can be over 1 ft (30 cm) thick. By contrast, the bark of a mature beech tree, shown here, may be as little as 0.5 in (1 cm) thick over most of the trunk.

DOUBLE DEFENSE
Old bark, like this from a poplar, forms a double barrier - it is tough and it contains chemical defenses. Some of these chemicals are used by people: the Peruvian cinchona tree, for example, provides quinine, used for treating malaria.

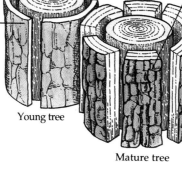

Bark cambium

New bark

Old cracked bark

Young tree

Mature tree

HOW BARK AGES
The bark of an ash sapling is smooth. As the tree matures, the bark develops many cracks and fissures.

HOW BARK GROWS
Every year, the bark cambium produces a new layer of bark which pushes the previous year's bark outward. The oldest bark is at the outside.

Natural cork oak bark

Cork tile

Bottle corks

Bark from a 60-year-old ash

STRIPPING CORK
Cork is the bark of the cork oak. Every eight or ten years, the outer bark of the trunk is stripped away to leave the bark cambium. This layer then grows into new bark.

THE PAST PRESERVED
Because it has a distinctive pattern, bark, like pollen, can be used to identify trees from the past. This piece of hazel bark is about 4,000 years old. The tree that produced it grew near a marshy area, and after it died it was covered by peat. Acids in the peat, and the lack of oxygen, kept it from decaying.

RESISTING DECAY
The papery bark of birches is very durable. As a result, bark from the North American paper birch was once used by Indians for making canoes.

IRREGULAR CRACKING
below
This strip of horse chestnut bark comes from a tree about 100 years old. Like the ash, the horse chestnut has bark that is smooth in a young tree, but which cracks as the tree ages. It splits into small, irregular plates as growth forces the bark outward.

MAPLE SYRUP
The early settlers in America were quick to take advantage of the sugar maple - a source of delicious syrup. To make the syrup, sap is first collected by pushing a hollow tube through the dead bark to the sap-conducting layer. The sap is boiled until only the sticky syrup remains.

PERFUMED BARK
The spice cinnamon is made from the bark of a tree that grows in India and Sri Lanka. Sticks of cinnamon are produced by cutting bark off young saplings; when left to dry, the bark curls up.

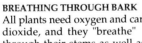

TRAPPED IN TIME
This wasp and a fly became stuck in pine resin oozing from bark 50 million years ago. Fossilized resin like this is known as amber.

THE FIREFIGHTER
The bark of the sequoia is thick and fibrous, and because it lacks resin, it does not easily catch fire. These two characteristics help to protect the huge tree from the forest blazes that kill so many other conifers.

BREATHING THROUGH BARK
All plants need oxygen and carbon dioxide, and they "breathe" through their stems as well as their leaves. This cherry wood shows the enlarged pores, or lenticels, which allow gases to penetrate through to the wood beneath.

FLAKING BARK
Many conifers, including the yews, spruces, and pines, have bark that flakes off in small pieces as the tree grows. On this yew trunk, patches of darker old bark have fallen away to reveal light red bark underneath.

Deep crack

Ivy

Lenticel through which the tree "breathes"

From bud to leaf

Horse chestnut buds

FOR ANY PLANT, growth is a demanding business. Even in tropical rain forests, where the climate is ideal for growth all year round, very few trees can grow nonstop. In higher latitudes, growth is stopped every year by the cold and darkness of winter, and resumes as buds burst in spring. Winter buds contain the materials that a tree needs to grow quickly once spring is under way. They can be found on all deciduous broadleaved trees, and on many conifers as well, although conifer buds are less easy to see among evergreen foliage. Each tree's buds follow a different plan. In some trees, the buds contain all the cells needed for the following season's growth; in others, they contain just the foundations for the following year, with the cells dividing rapidly once the buds have burst. Trees can be identified, even in winter, by the shape and arrangement of the buds.

Leading bud with scales partly folded back as it begins to burst

Paired lateral buds

Leaf scar

ONE YEAR AGO
Last year's growth extends from the leading bud back to the girdle scar. The length of twig between these points shows that it was a good year for growth.

THE HORSE CHESTNUT
Each of the horse chestnut's large, sticky buds contains the tightly packed material for an entire season's growth. When the days lengthen in early spring, the resinous coating on the bud melts, and the protective scales spring back. The cells within the bud expand rapidly. Within the space of two weeks, the shoot can grow by as much as 18 in (45 cm). The leading buds - the ones at the tip of a shoot - contain tightly packed flowers as well as leaves. The lateral buds (ones on the sides of the branches) contain only leaves. When they emerge from the bud, horse chestnut flowers and leaves are covered in a protective down.

Immature leaves

Bud scales

Immature stem

INSIDE A BUD
A bud contains immature leaves folded inside a protective case. Although trees with large leaves often have large buds, this is not always so.

One-year-old side shoot formed from lateral bud at tip of twig

Dormant (inactive) buds begin to grow only if the growing buds are damaged

Girdle scar shows where one season's growth ended and the next began

Three-year-old side shoot formed from lateral bud at tip of twig

Girdle scar

TWO YEARS AGO
The twig did not grow very long and did not produce any side shoots.

THREE YEARS AGO
During this year, the twig did not grow a great deal. The twig produced a side shoot which is now three years old.

"WITCH'S BROOMS"
Uncontrolled growth of buds may be set off by infections; this is often seen in birches.

24

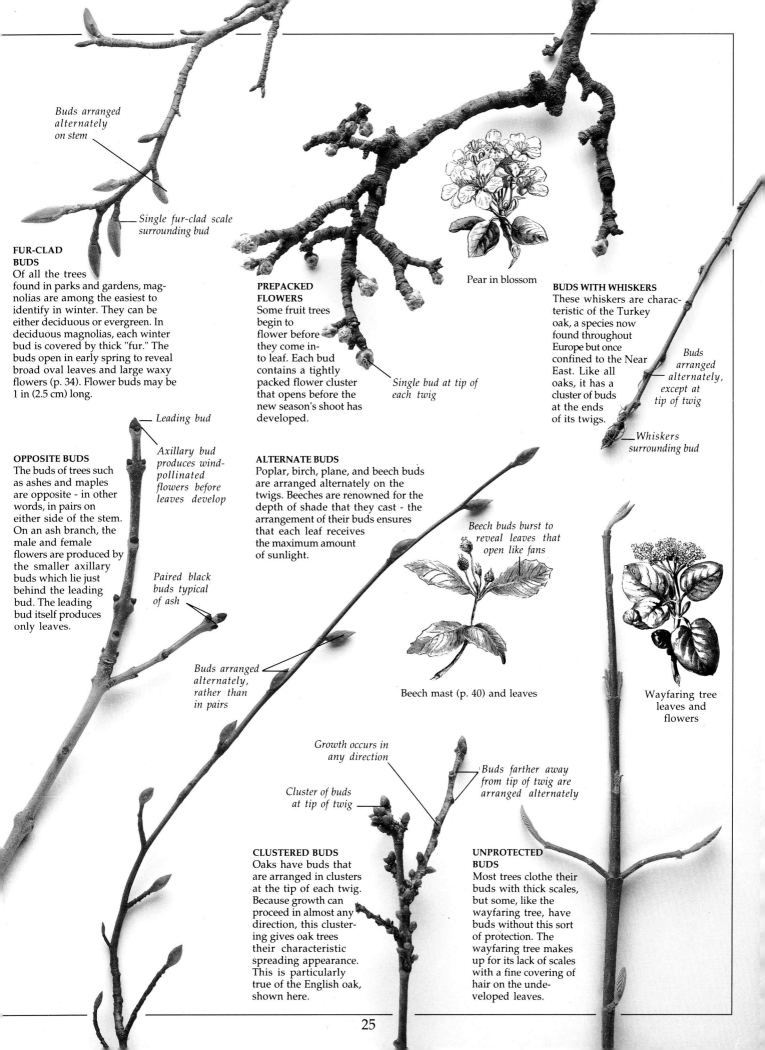

FUR-CLAD BUDS
Of all the trees found in parks and gardens, magnolias are among the easiest to identify in winter. They can be either deciduous or evergreen. In deciduous magnolias, each winter bud is covered by thick "fur." The buds open in early spring to reveal broad oval leaves and large waxy flowers (p. 34). Flower buds may be 1 in (2.5 cm) long.

Buds arranged alternately on stem

Single fur-clad scale surrounding bud

PREPACKED FLOWERS
Some fruit trees begin to flower before they come into leaf. Each bud contains a tightly packed flower cluster that opens before the new season's shoot has developed.

Single bud at tip of each twig

Pear in blossom

BUDS WITH WHISKERS
These whiskers are characteristic of the Turkey oak, a species now found throughout Europe but once confined to the Near East. Like all oaks, it has a cluster of buds at the ends of its twigs.

Buds arranged alternately, except at tip of twig

Whiskers surrounding bud

OPPOSITE BUDS
The buds of trees such as ashes and maples are opposite - in other words, in pairs on either side of the stem. On an ash branch, the male and female flowers are produced by the smaller axillary buds which lie just behind the leading bud. The leading bud itself produces only leaves.

Leading bud

Axillary bud produces wind-pollinated flowers before leaves develop

Paired black buds typical of ash

ALTERNATE BUDS
Poplar, birch, plane, and beech buds are arranged alternately on the twigs. Beeches are renowned for the depth of shade that they cast - the arrangement of their buds ensures that each leaf receives the maximum amount of sunlight.

Beech buds burst to reveal leaves that open like fans

Buds arranged alternately, rather than in pairs

Beech mast (p. 40) and leaves

Wayfaring tree leaves and flowers

Growth occurs in any direction

Cluster of buds at tip of twig

Buds farther away from tip of twig are arranged alternately

CLUSTERED BUDS
Oaks have buds that are arranged in clusters at the tip of each twig. Because growth can proceed in almost any direction, this clustering gives oak trees their characteristic spreading appearance. This is particularly true of the English oak, shown here.

UNPROTECTED BUDS
Most trees clothe their buds with thick scales, but some, like the wayfaring tree, have buds without this sort of protection. The wayfaring tree makes up for its lack of scales with a fine covering of hair on the undeveloped leaves.

Simple leaves

THE LEAVES OF A TREE are like miniature power stations, but instead of burning fuel, they generate it. They take in energy in the form of sunlight and use it to turn carbon dioxide and water into sugars. These sugars can then be used as a fuel, or they can make cellulose, the substance that forms the tree's cells and on which the wood-forming substance, lignin, is laid down. The leaves of broad-leaved trees can be divided into two types - simple and compound (p. 28).

Veins spread out across the leaf blade in a network

Microscopic pores on surface of leaf allow gases to enter

Leaf blade

Midrib

Close-up of a simple broadleaf

Stalk or petiole

White willow

Osier

LANCE-LEAVED WILLOWS
Many willows have long narrow leaves with silvery hairs on the undersides.

Jagged teeth around edge of leaf

TOOTHED OVAL LEAVES
The shape of the cultivated cherry leaf is common to many trees.

Upper surface, covered in fine hairs

YOUNG GIANT
The oval leaves of some magnolias can grow up to 1 ft (30 cm) long. This specimen is a young leaf.

HEART-SHAPED LEAVES
Symmetrical (even) heart-shaped leaves are uncommon in the tree world: the redbud and the katsura are two garden species that have them. This leaf is from the redbud.

UNEQUAL LOBES
Leaves with unequal lobes are grown by basswoods. In summer they may become covered with honeydew produced by sap-sucking insects.

VARIEGATED LEAVES
In most leaves the green pigment chlorophyll, which harnesses the energy of sunlight, is spread throughout the leaf. In a variegated (multicolored) leaf, it is reduced or absent in parts. These leaves cannot trap much sunlight and rarely survive.

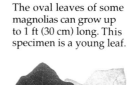

Smooth, dark upper surface

Underside

SOFT UNDERSIDES
The round leaves of the gray poplar have pale, downy undersides.

SAW-TOOTHED CHESTNUTS
The sweet chestnut's jagged, tough leaves are a familiar sight in Europe. The same distinctive leaves were once well known in North America until chestnut blight destroyed all the trees.

Copper beech descended from a natural mutation

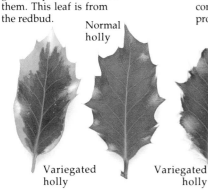

Normal holly

Variegated holly

Variegated holly

Cultivated Japanese maple

UNUSUAL PIGMENTS
Dark-colored leaves contain the green pigment chlorophyll, but it is masked by various other pigments.

Cultivated Japanese maple

Young leaf emerging
from sheath on
growing shoot

*Central notch
divides leaf
in two*

English oak

VARIABLE SHAPES
Most deciduous oaks have lobed
or toothed leaves, which are
usually leathery to the touch.
Evergreen oaks are quite different -
many of them have short, lance-
shaped leaves.

Red
oak

White
oak

Two-pointed
leaf

ODD TREE OUT
The two species of tulip tree - one
North American and the other
Chinese - have large, flat-ended
leaves that are quite unlike those
of any other tree. The specimen
shown here is a young leaf with two
points. Large mature leaves usually
have four points (p. 37), which can
be arranged in a variety of ways.

*Parallel
veins*

ANCIENT SURVIVOR
The primitive ginkgo's
fanlike leaves have
remained unchanged
for over 200 million
years. Once known
only in China, this
tree is now grown
in parks and
gardens all over
the world.

Vine-leaved
Japanese maple

**HANDLIKE
LEAVES**
Maple leaves are
generally easy to
recognize by their
handlike shapes. How-
ever, some species, such
as the snake-bark or moose-bark
maples of China, Japan and North
America, can be confusing at first:
many have scarcely lobed leaves.
The leaves of another maple, box
elder, are compound (pp. 28-29).

Snake-bark
maple

Japanese maple

CITY DWELLERS
Although plane leaves are hand-
shaped, planes are not related to
maples, as their fruits (p. 41)
clearly show. Plane leaves have
a tough, glossy surface that
is washed clean by rain,
helping them to grow well
even in the polluted air
of cities.

LATE INTO LEAF
Catalpas, or Indian
bean trees, have some
of the largest of all
simple deciduous
leaves, reaching 1 ft
(30 cm) in length.
Catalapas are natives
of the subtropics. When
they are grown in
cooler climates the
leaves do not reach full
size until midsummer.

Mature catalpa

27

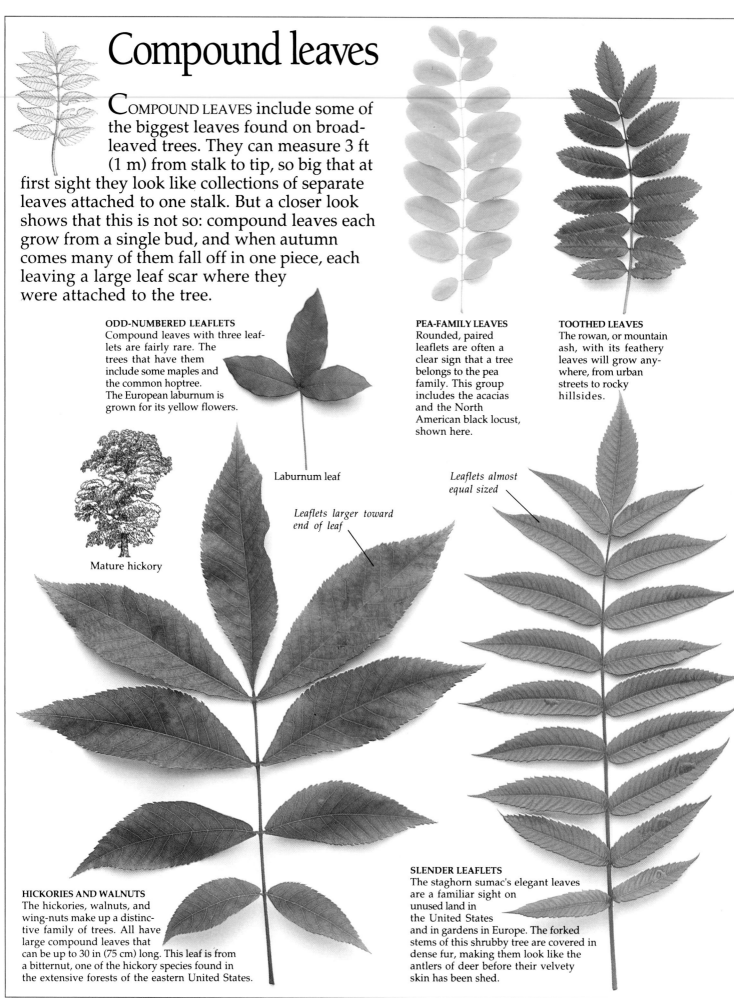

Compound leaves

COMPOUND LEAVES include some of the biggest leaves found on broad-leaved trees. They can measure 3 ft (1 m) from stalk to tip, so big that at first sight they look like collections of separate leaves attached to one stalk. But a closer look shows that this is not so: compound leaves each grow from a single bud, and when autumn comes many of them fall off in one piece, each leaving a large leaf scar where they were attached to the tree.

ODD-NUMBERED LEAFLETS
Compound leaves with three leaflets are fairly rare. The trees that have them include some maples and the common hoptree. The European laburnum is grown for its yellow flowers.

Mature hickory

Laburnum leaf

Leaflets larger toward end of leaf

PEA-FAMILY LEAVES
Rounded, paired leaflets are often a clear sign that a tree belongs to the pea family. This group includes the acacias and the North American black locust, shown here.

TOOTHED LEAVES
The rowan, or mountain ash, with its feathery leaves will grow anywhere, from urban streets to rocky hillsides.

Leaflets almost equal sized

HICKORIES AND WALNUTS
The hickories, walnuts, and wing-nuts make up a distinctive family of trees. All have large compound leaves that can be up to 30 in (75 cm) long. This leaf is from a bitternut, one of the hickory species found in the extensive forests of the eastern United States.

SLENDER LEAFLETS
The staghorn sumac's elegant leaves are a familiar sight on unused land in the United States and in gardens in Europe. The forked stems of this shrubby tree are covered in dense fur, making them look like the antlers of deer before their velvety skin has been shed.

Horse chestnut leaf

Mature ash tree in leaf

*Leaflets arranged
in a circle*

SHORT-STAY LEAVES
In Europe, the commonest large tree with compound leaves is the ash. Though large, ash leaves are sparse, and even a big ash tree casts little shade. In the autumn the ash is slow to shed its foliage. According to folklore the ash tree possessed medicinal powers, and it was believed that a sick child would be cured if he or she was passed through the branches of the ash.

PALMATE LEAVES
The leaves of all the horse chestnut family have leaflets that point outward like the fingers of a hand. The horse chestnut has seven or nine leaflets, while its relatives, the North American buckeyes, usually have five.

Hercules-club

DOUBLY DIVIDED
The Hercules-club from North America has enormous leaves that are twice compound: each leaflet is attached to a side stalk. The leaves may be over 3 ft (1 m) long and almost as wide. Doubly divided leaves are very unusual among trees. Only one other tree with them, also from North America, is at all common. This is the Kentucky coffee tree - not a relative of the true coffee bush but a member of the pea family. Its seeds were used as a coffee sub-stitute during the last century.

*Leaflets paired and
of equal size*

29

Needles and scales

THE NEEDLES AND SCALES OF CONIFERS are quite unlike the leaves of broadleaved trees. They have parallel veins and a hard or leathery surface. With a few exceptions, such as larches, they remain on the tree all the year round. Including the yews, there are seven families of conifers, and the most important are the pines, redwoods, and cypresses. Pine-family conifers include not only pines but also firs, spruces, cedars, and larches. Conifers have a variety of leaf shapes. Pines, cedars, and larches, for example, have needles; firs, yews, and some redwoods have flattened, leathery leaves; and cypresses have scales.

ORNAMENTAL CONIFERS
Many species of conifers have been bred for their ornamental foliage, which can be green, yellow, or even blue. These feathery scales are from a cultivated sawara cypress.

Blue atlas cedar

Blue-green needles of cultivated blue atlas cedar

NEEDLES IN ROSETTES
A number of conifers are known as cedars - but not all are true cedars. Evergreen needles that grow in rosettes identify this group.

Needles in pairs

Scotch pine

Needles in fives

Arolla pine

NEEDLES IN BUNCHES
Pines all have long needles that grow in bunches of two, three, or five. Each needle has a thick outer layer, or cuticle, and a coating of wax. Together, these reduce water loss and allow pines to live in places that are too dry for many other conifers.

Flat, dark green needles

Needles in threes

Monterey pine

LEAVES FOR ALL SEASONS
Firs have tough, flat leaves. Like many other conifers, they are adapted to cope with heavy falls of snow. Their sloping branches and smooth, flexible leaves shed snow easily without breaking under its weight. The leaves have a built-in "antifreeze" and are not damaged by frost.

Underside of silver fir

GRAVEYARD SENTINEL
The yew's dark foliage is poisonous. Often planted in churchyards, yews have become a symbol of death.

Many fir leaves are differently colored above and below

Upper side of silver fir

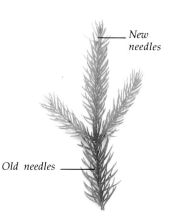

New needles

Old needles

Hard, triangular leaves with spiked tips

Monkey puzzle

THE COPPICING CONIFER
The California redwood or sequoia produces sprouts from its stump after felling, just as in a coppiced broadleaved tree (p. 61).

NEEDLES ON PEGS
Spruces have spiky needles that grow from small "pegs" on their twigs. Christmas trees are usually Norway spruces; when they lose their needles, the leaf pegs are easy to see.

SCALES AROUND THE STEM
The Japanese cedar has small scalelike leaves around its stems. Despite its name, it is a redwood, not a cedar.

UNIQUE APPEARANCE
The monkey puzzle is almost impossible to mistake. Also known as the Chile pine, it is actually not a pine but one of an unusual family of conifers found mainly in South America and Australia. It is grown as an ornamental tree in many parts of Europe and North America.

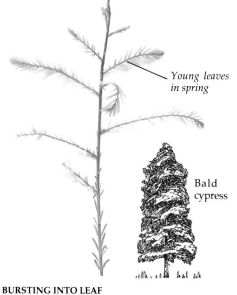

Young leaves in spring

Bald cypress

Soft, flexible needles are shed every autumn

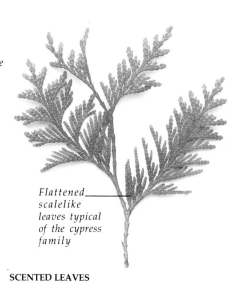

Flattened scalelike leaves typical of the cypress family

BURSTING INTO LEAF
The bald cypress (p. 18) is a deciduous redwood, like its distant cousin the dawn redwood (below). Bald cypress leaves are yellowish when they emerge in spring but become dark green as they mature.

THE DECIDUOUS CONIFER
Larches (a family that includes the tamarack) can grow in the coldest climates. Their needles are in rosettes and are shed in autumn.

SCENTED LEAVES
Thujas are members of the cypress family. The western red cedar is a thuja. It is easy to identify because when its leaves are crushed, they smell like pineapple. Many other conifers have scented leaves; giant fir, for example, smells like oranges.

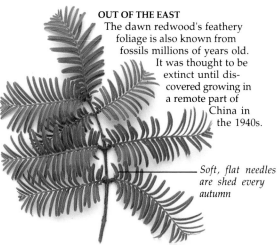

OUT OF THE EAST
The dawn redwood's feathery foliage is also known from fossils millions of years old. It was thought to be extinct until discovered growing in a remote part of China in the 1940s.

Soft, flat needles are shed every autumn

A CONTRAST IN SCALE
Although the giant sequoia is one of the world's biggest trees, it has some of the smallest leaves. Its tiny scales are packed tightly around the stems.

TWO TYPES OF LEAVES
Some junipers have spiky leaves when young and scalelike leaves when adult. The common juniper, shown here, has only spiky leaves. Cultivated junipers have leaves that are all shades of green, yellow, and blue.

Blowing in the wind

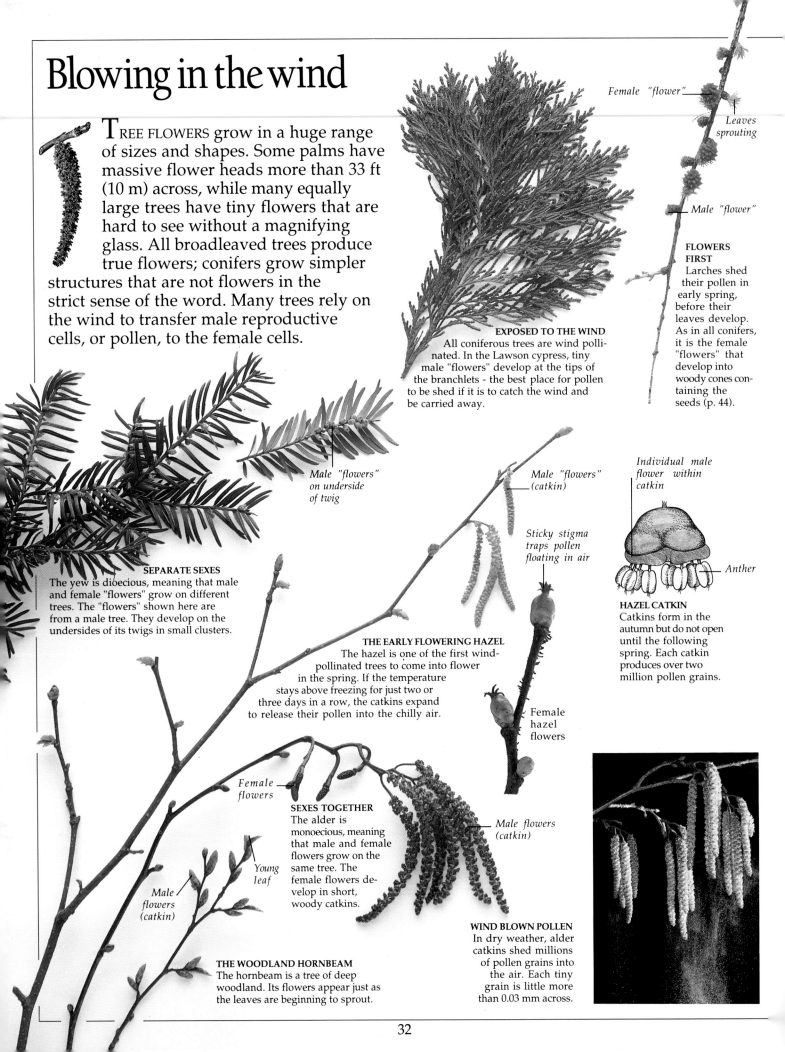

TREE FLOWERS grow in a huge range of sizes and shapes. Some palms have massive flower heads more than 33 ft (10 m) across, while many equally large trees have tiny flowers that are hard to see without a magnifying glass. All broadleaved trees produce true flowers; conifers grow simpler structures that are not flowers in the strict sense of the word. Many trees rely on the wind to transfer male reproductive cells, or pollen, to the female cells.

EXPOSED TO THE WIND
All coniferous trees are wind polli-nated. In the Lawson cypress, tiny male "flowers" develop at the tips of the branchlets - the best place for pollen to be shed if it is to catch the wind and be carried away.

Female "flower"

Leaves sprouting

Male "flower"

FLOWERS FIRST
Larches shed their pollen in early spring, before their leaves develop. As in all conifers, it is the female "flowers" that develop into woody cones con-taining the seeds (p. 44).

Male "flowers" on underside of twig

SEPARATE SEXES
The yew is dioecious, meaning that male and female "flowers" grow on different trees. The "flowers" shown here are from a male tree. They develop on the undersides of its twigs in small clusters.

Male "flowers" (catkin)

Sticky stigma traps pollen floating in air

Individual male flower within catkin

Anther

HAZEL CATKIN
Catkins form in the autumn but do not open until the following spring. Each catkin produces over two million pollen grains.

THE EARLY FLOWERING HAZEL
The hazel is one of the first wind-pollinated trees to come into flower in the spring. If the temperature stays above freezing for just two or three days in a row, the catkins expand to release their pollen into the chilly air.

Female hazel flowers

Female flowers

Young leaf

SEXES TOGETHER
The alder is monoecious, meaning that male and female flowers grow on the same tree. The female flowers de-velop in short, woody catkins.

Male flowers (catkin)

Male flowers (catkin)

THE WOODLAND HORNBEAM
The hornbeam is a tree of deep woodland. Its flowers appear just as the leaves are beginning to sprout.

WIND BLOWN POLLEN
In dry weather, alder catkins shed millions of pollen grains into the air. Each tiny grain is little more than 0.03 mm across.

Growing shoot

Cluster of male "flowers"

CLUES FROM THE PAST
Pollen grains are very resilient. Scientists can discover what trees grew where from pollen preserved in peat deposits.

Cluster of female flowers

POLLEN WITH SAILS
Pines produce enormous numbers of pollen grains, and if the male "flowers" are given a sharp knock, a cloud of yellow pollen appears. Pine pollen grains have two tiny air-filled sacs attached to them, and these act like sails to carry the grains far through the air.

POLLEN IN THE STREETS
Ornamental plane trees shed huge quantities of pollen into towns and cities in spring. Both the male and female flower clusters are ball-shaped, and they hang from the tree in small groups.

Cluster of male Scotch pine "flowers"

BEDRAGGLED CATKINS
The unimpressive, straggly catkins of the English oak open in late spring in un-tidy bunches. The female flowers, destined to produce the acorns, are clustered at the tips of the shoots.

Catkin divided into three branches

Female flowers on stalks, a characteristic feature of English oak

Catkin

BRANCHED CATKINS
Hickories shed their pollen in early summer from catkins that are branched into three. The female flowers, which are at the tips of the shoots, are not at all noticeable.

Stigma of female flower

NEW AND OLD GROWTH
The walnut's catkins sprout from the previous year's shoot. The much smaller female flowers, whose sticky stigmas can be seen here, develop at the end of the new shoot.

Insect-pollinated flowers

By FAR THE MOST NOTICEABLE TREE FLOWERS are those that are pollinated by animals, usually insects. Insect-pollinated flowers have evolved supplies of sugar-rich nectar which draw bees, butterflies, beetles, flies, and countless other insects to them. The pollen grains of these trees are bigger than those of wind-pollinated flowers - up to .012 in (0.3 mm) across. They also have a sticky coating that makes them cling to an insect's body so that they can be transferred from one tree to another.

ATTRACTING BY SCENT
The bird cherry attracts insects not only by color but by smell. Like many insect-pollinated plants, the flowers produce an almond-like perfume.

Stigma (female)

Anther (male)

Insects transfer pollen from male anthers to the female ovule via the stigma

Ovule (female)

Flower made up of fleshy scales

After pollination, flowers droop - this clears a path for bees toward unpollinated flowers

KANZAN CHERRY
The Kanzan Japanese cherry is one of the most popular varieties in cultivation. Huge clusters of flowers weigh down its branches in spring, but this variety never produces fruit. The elaborate flowers have been so highly bred for decoration that their reproductive structures no longer work.

AN ANCIENT LINEAGE
The first flowers to appear on Earth belonged to magnolia-like plants, and their cuplike blooms have probably changed little in 200 million years. The petals are set in a spiral around a central point containing the male anthers and female stigma.

A WEALTH OF BREEDING
Over the centuries, a handful of species of wild cherry have been bred to produce hundreds of ornamental varieties. Japanese flowering cherries probably came from four wild species.

Double ring of petals found only in cultivated varieties

Anthers and stigma reduced in size

Double ring of petals

ORNAMENTAL APPLE
Apples have been cultivated since Roman times not only for their fruit (p. 39) but also for their flowers. Like all apples, the delicate flowers of this ornamental crab have five petals that sit on a cup known as a receptacle. After the flower has been pollinated by visiting insects, the receptacle swells to produce the outer flesh of the fruit.

Ring of five petals

ONE SEX AT A TIME
The blackthorn, or sloe, is a shrub or small tree that flowers before it comes into leaf. As in many flowers, the stigma matures before the anthers release their sticky pollen. This keeps the flower from pollinating itself.

Clusters of flowers on spiny side branches

Encrusting lichen

ALL MIXED UP
The horse chestnut is pollinated by bees. Each flower head is made up of a mixture of flower types: some are entirely male, and others have both male and female parts. Only the second type can produce "conkers."

Ripe anthers covered in pollen

MIXED ORCHARDS
The flowers of most apple varieties will produce fruit only if they receive pollen from a different variety. By planting rows of different varieties together, apple growers are able to ensure that bees carry pollen from one variety to another.

Animal-pollinated flowers

THE FLOWERS of many trees are specially adapted to lure animal visitors. These animals distribute pollen in return for a meal of nectar, a sugary liquid produced by the flower. The flowers attract their pollinators by their color and scent, and they are shaped so that the animal cannot avoid being dusted with pollen. Although insects are the most important of these pollinators, in some areas birds and bats also carry pollen and so help to produce seeds.

Each flower has five petals; the lowest pair forms a projecting "keel" that springs open when an insect lands on it

SPRING-LOADED FLOWERS
The flowers of the redbud are arranged so that the weight of a visiting insect makes them spring open. This ensures that pollen sticks to the insect and is carried off.

Judas tree in flower

TINY FLOWERS
Maples have clusters of nectar-rich flowers that appear before the leaves or at the same time. Each tiny flower has a ring of pollen-producing stamens. This flower cluster is from a sycamore, a kind of maple.

LANDING PLATFORM
Small flowers packed closely together, like those of the rowan, provide insects with a convenient landing platform.

Wild hawthorn

Cultivated hawthorn with double ring of petals

BLAZE OF COLOR
Hawthorns produce heavily scented flowers. According to legend, one hawthorn, the Glastonbury thorn, was brought to England by St. Joseph of Aramathea. It is unusual in that it flowers twice a year.

Bract

Flower

Flower bud

Flower beginning to open with sepals folding back

FALSE PETALS
In most flowers it is the petals that are large and noticeable and so attract pollinators. But some flowers have evolved other ways of getting attention. This flower is from a North American dogwood. The four structures that look like petals are in fact special leaves called bracts which attract insects to the tiny flower.

Showy petals at mouth of flower

Tube leading to nectar

Circle of six petals

Sepals folded back

NAMED FOR ITS SHAPE
The tulip tree is related to the magnolias (p. 34). It gets its name from its cup-shaped flowers, which, like those of magnolias, are large and have a central spire.

Upper and lower half of beak form a narrow tube for drinking nectar

BIRD POLLINATION
In the Americas, hummingbirds pollinate many species of plants, including some trees. The birds' long beaks reach deep into the flowers to obtain nectar.

TUBULAR FLOWERS
The flowers of the catalpa, or Indian bean tree, are shaped so that a visiting insect has to crawl deep inside a tube to reach the nectar. In doing so, it is dusted with pollen.

Hairs at tip of tongue form a brush to collect pollen

BAT POLLINATION
Bat-pollinated trees include the baobab and kapok (p. 43). Both of these trees have big flowers that produce large quantities of nectar, especially at night. Bats eat both pollen and nectar, and in doing so transfer pollen from one flower to another on their tongues and noses. Most tree-pollinating bats hover in front of the flowers; they use the same technique as hummingbirds but are much less acrobatic.

INSECT LURE
Elder flowers have a powerful smell that insects, especially hover flies, find highly attractive. This perfume can be noticed in elder flower wine, which is made by collecting the flowers as soon as they open and before their smell becomes sour.

Fruit and berries

FORBIDDEN FRUIT
Fruit has often been associated with temptation. Although the fruit that caused Adam and Eve's fall is often said to be an apple, the Bible just refers to it as a fruit.

AFTER A TREE'S FLOWERS have been pollinated, the female part of the flower produces the seeds. Trees are faced with the same problem in scattering their seeds as in scattering their pollen: the trees themselves cannot move, so they need the help of something that can. To get around this problem, many produce brightly colored, tasty fruit that attracts animals, particularly birds. In return for a meal, a bird will unknowingly scatter seeds far and wide in its droppings as it flies from tree to tree. New trees spring up where the seeds fall.

Small seed surrounded by a fleshy jacket, known as an aril

CHEMICAL COLORS
Red berries, like those of the rowan, are colored by carotenoids. These get their name because they also color carrots orange.

POISONOUS FRUIT
Yews, like junipers, are conifers, but they are unusual in producing juicy, colored "berries" like those of broadleaved trees. When a bird feeds on the bright red fruit, the fleshy aril is digested but the seed, which is poisonous, passes through its body intact.

MIDSUMMER MULBERRY
Greek legend has it that the mulberry's fruit was stained red by the blood of Pyramus, the lover who also appears in Shakespeare's *A Midsummer Night's Dream.*

Ripening black mulberry

Ripe black mulberry

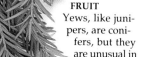

MIDWINTER FOOD
Hawthorn berries are a vital food for birds in winter. They remain on the tree long after most other hedgerow berries have disappeared.

Silkworm caterpillars feed only on white mulberry leaves

Mulberries hanging down beneath leaves

THE TENACIOUS ELDER
Elderberries are often eaten by birds. The seeds that fall in their droppings can germinate and grow with almost no soil. They are often seen growing out of houses, where a seed has germinated in a wall.

Cultivated fruit

Since tree seeds were first deliberately planted, gardeners have spent centuries improving and adapting fruit to human needs by selective breeding. The apple is a good example of the changes that cultivation has made. Wild apples, which are still found in woods and shrublands, are small and bitter and relished by birds but not by humans. Over a thousand cultivated varieties have been produced, all much larger and sweeter than their wild counterparts. This has been achieved by continually selecting seeds from the most promising trees, and by crossing one tree with another in the hope of combining the best of their characteristics.

SCIENCE AND THE APPLE
Apple breeders, or pomologists, use the science of genetics to produce apples that taste good and that are easy to pick. Modern apple trees can be cropped when they are saplings only a yard or so high.

The "Worcester pearmain" - a modern variety

The "russet" - an old, established variety with a thick, rough skin

Fleshy layer develops around the base of the pollinated flower

Seeds

Single, hard stone typical of plum fruit

Pear

Seed

Nectarine

Boundary of seed compartment

FROM STONE TO FRUIT
Like all plums, damsons are easy to grow from their stones. These are some of the smallest cultivated plums.

OUT OF THE WILD
Most cultivated plums are the descendants of two wild shrubs, the blackthorn, or sloe (p. 35), and the cherry plum.

FAMILY LIKENESS
The plums include not only true plums but also cherries, peaches, apricots, nectarines, and almonds.

DIVIDED UP
Inside the fruit the seed compartment of apples and pears is divided into sections, each containing one or two seeds.

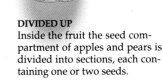

THE CITRUS FRUITS
Citrus fruits like oranges and lemons contain fruit sugars and citric acid. In lemons, the acid outweighs the sugars, giving the fruit a sharp flavor.

SWEET AND SOUR
Oranges originally came from Asia. The sweet orange, used for eating, and the Seville or sour orange, used for marmalade, are two different species.

Seed compartments visible at flat end of fruit

THE ANCIENT OLIVE
Botanically speaking, the olive is a fruit. It has been cultivated for its rich oil for thousands of years.

STAPLE DIET
Thrushes, blackbirds, and many other birds rely on berries to survive the winter.

THE MEDLAR
Like the apple, the seed compartment of the medlar is divided up into five sections. Medlars are usually eaten only when they begin to rot.

Seeds and nuts

TREES DISPERSE THEIR SEEDS in a number of ways: some wrap them up in berries that are tempting to birds (p. 38); others produce seeds inside tough cases. The seeds, together with their cases, make up the trees' fruit. The exact shape of the seedcase depends on how the seed is dispersed - whether by mammals, wind, or water. Some trees, such as walnuts and beeches, produce big, well-protected seeds. These are carried away by hungry mammals such as squirrels, and although some seeds are eaten, a number survive and germinate. Other trees have seeds inside winged cases that are carried by the wind. A few riverside trees, such as the alder, use water to disperse their seeds. The case of an alder seed contains a droplet of oil that makes it float, so the seed is swept away downstream by the current to germinate when it arrives on a muddy bank.

SEED CATKINS
In late summer, wing-nut trees, which come from Asia and Japan, are covered in giant catkins hanging down from their branches. These are in fact long clusters in cases with flaps. The short flaps probably help to dislodge the seeds once ripe.

Filberts

BEECH BANQUET
Once a year, beech trees produce mast, or beech-nuts. In the past, pigs were often turned loose beneath beech trees to fatten on the oil-rich seeds.

COBS AND FILBERTS
Cultivated hazelnuts are sold as "cobnuts." Filberts, which are larger, come from a hazel that grows in southeastern Europe.

SEEDS ON THREADS
The seeds of the cucumber tree, a type of magnolia, show up as round swellings in a bright red pod. Each swelling splits open to reveal a brilliant red seed suspended on a silk-like thread.

SMALL NUTS
Pistachios come from a small Asian tree that is now grown around the Mediterranean and in the southern United States.

Prickly case protects developing nuts

Horse chestnut cases are usually spiny

Roasting chestnuts

WINTER WARMER
Roasted sweet chestnuts are tasty and nutritious. The best nuts grow in warm climates, such as in Spain and California.

SHINY "CONKERS"
Horse chestnuts, or "conkers," are slightly poisonous to humans. Other mammals, especially deer, cattle, and sheep, can eat large quantities of them without suffering any ill effects.

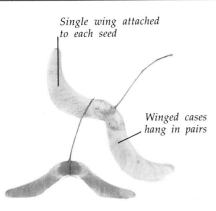

Single wing attached to each seed

Winged cases hang in pairs

WINGED MAPLE SEEDS
Maples have seeds in winged cases. When the cases fall, they spiral to the ground like miniature helicopters.

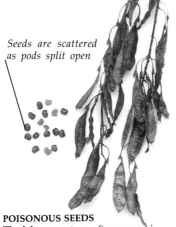

Seeds are scattered as pods split open

POISONOUS SEEDS
The laburnum tree, often grown in gardens, has highly poisonous seeds. As in all pea-family trees, the seeds grow in pods.

Ash keys often remain on tree throughout the winter

FLYING KEYS
Completely female ash trees produce winged "keys" and, in some years bear them on all branches. However, male trees have no keys. In trees with both male and female branches, only the female ones bear keys.

BASSWOOD NUTLETS
Basswood trees have small bunches of fragrant, yellowish flowers. After these have been pollinated, each flower produces a furry nut containing the small seeds.

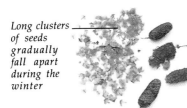

Long clusters of seeds gradually fall apart during the winter

FIRST ARRIVAL
Each birch seed is enclosed in a case with two tiny wings. The fruits are light enough to be blown long distances, so birches appear quickly on unused ground.

Unripe seedhead

Ripe acorns of Turkey oak

Healthy unripe acorn

EDIBLE SEEDS
Most oaks do not begin to produce acorns until they are about 50 years old. To a botanist, acorns are in fact nuts, but they are not commonly called nuts because people rarely eat them. However, they used to be the staple food of one tribe of Indians in California who ground them down into flour.

Acorn cup deformed into a gall by larva of gall wasp

"SPORTING" SEEDS
The tulip tree's seeds grow in a pointed seedhead. At first, the cluster is green, but gradually it turns brown and opens to look like a shuttlecock. The seedhead falls apart a year after flowering.

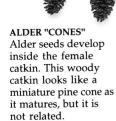

ALDER "CONES"
Alder seeds develop inside the female catkin. This woody catkin looks like a miniature pine cone as it matures, but it is not related.

THE SQUIRREL'S HIDDEN STORES
Squirrels eat many seeds and bury others to provide food for the winter. The ones that the squirrels haven't eaten germinate when spring arrives.

Skin surrounding nut

Woody shell

Edible kernel

COLORED SKINS
On the tree, a walnut is covered by a green skin that gradually turns black, collapses, and releases the nut. The walnut is enclosed in a hard shell that keeps out animals.

AMERICAN FAVORITE
The pecan is one of the most important edible nuts from North America. It is produced by a tree related to the walnut, and its nuts taste very similar to walnuts.

HAIRY IRRITANTS
Plane tree seeds grow in ball-shaped clusters that stay on the tree all winter. In spring they burst open, releasing the seeds and millions of tiny golden hairs. These hairs can have an eye-watering effect on anyone who encounters them.

41

Tropical fruit and nuts

T ROPICAL TREES that produce edible fruit and nuts have been bred by people since ancient times. The date palm, for example, is known to have been cultivated for at least 5,000 years. People have also carried countless species from one place to another to provide food. Examples include the papaya, avocado pear, and cocoa, which originally grew in South America, and the mango, which came from Asia. Perhaps the most famous of these tropical travelers is breadfruit. During the first attempt to transport it from the South Seas to the West Indies, the crew of the ship carrying it, HMS *Bounty*, mutinied against the notorious Captain Bligh.

The coconut palm - a tree that spreads by waterborne seeds

TAMARIND PODS
The Indian tamarind tree is a member of the pea family (p. 28), and, like all its relatives, it produces seeds in pods. The flesh around the seeds is a valuable spice, and the pods are also a traditional medicine.

Dried nutmeg

NUTMEG AND MACE
The nutmeg tree provides two different spices. The first is nutmeg itself, which is the tree's seed. The second is mace, an intensely flavored, fleshy network that surrounds the seed.

THE SPICE TRADE
Many spices produced from tree seeds are used to flavor food.

Hard shell protects the nutritious kernel

Seeds and case together weigh up to 3.5 lb (1.5 kg)

Stalk attaches pot to tree

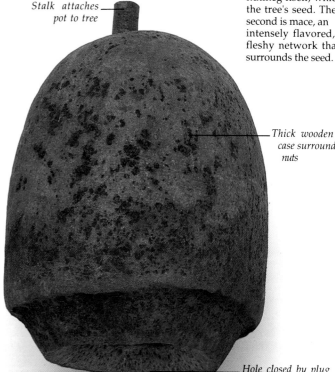

Thick wooden case surrounds nuts

BRAZIL NUT
These nuts come from the Amazonian rain forest. The trees on which they grow have never been successfully cultivated, so all Brazil nuts have to be gathered from wild trees. Collecting Brazil nuts is not easy. The trees are often very tall, and the nuts are contained in a hard wooden case which has to be smashed open.

Lightweight husk acts as a float

OCEAN WANDERERS
Many trees that grow on tropical coasts scatter their seeds by dropping them into the sea, where they are carried off by currents. Many eventually sink, but some do reach land far away from their original home and take root. This seed is from a tropical tree called *Barringtonia*. Its flowers open at night and wither at dawn.

Hole closed by plug

Monkeypot nuts

MONKEYPOT
The "monkeypot" tree is a relative of the Brazil nut. It produces its seeds in wooden cups that Indians once used for catching wild monkeys.

Plug

MEAT TENDERIZER
As well as being very sweet, the papaya (or papaw) is rich in papain, a substance that breaks down proteins. Papain is collected from papaya fruit and used to tenderize meat.

THE MANGO
Sweet-tasting mango fruit comes from trees that originally grew in southeast Asia. They are now cultivated throughout the tropics.

Date palms

Coconut germinating after a sea-crossing many months long

FRUIT FROM THE DESERT
Date palms are native to Africa and the Middle East. The fruit grows in hanging clusters, each containing up to 1,500 dates.

COCOA AND CHOCOLATE
It was the Aztecs who first made a substance they called *chocolatl*, or chocolate, from the seeds inside cocoa pods.

Baobab tree

THE SHRINKING TREE
The extraordinary baobab produces long, sausage-shaped pods packed with seeds rich in vitamin C. The baobab has a huge swollen trunk which is used to store water. In times of drought, the tree shrinks as this supply of water is used up.

THE WORLD'S BIGGEST SEED
The coco-de-mer's enormous nut weighs up to 45 lb (20 kg), making it the largest seed of any plant. Coco-de-mer grows only in the Seychelles islands. Its nuts are divided into two lobes and for this reason are sometimes called the "double coconut."

Hard seed-case

Fibers surrounding seeds

NATURAL FIBERS
Before the invention of artificial fibers, the fibers produced by the kapok tree were collected and sold for stuffing mattresses and furniture.

Cones

Crossbill feeding

COMPARED WITH MANY BROAD-LEAVED TREES, conifers take a long time to produce their seeds. During the months that the seeds take to develop, they are protected by a hard cone. In trees such as the pines, the cone falls off in one piece some time after the seeds have been shed. In others, such as the cedars, the cone falls apart on the tree, so it is hardly ever found whole on the ground.

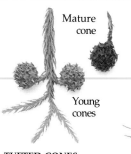

Mature cone

Young cones

TUFTED CONES
The cones of Japanese cedar are simple to identify because they are ball-shaped and each scale has a featherlike tuft projecting from it.

Young cones

Mature cone

AGE DIFFERENCES
When the larch's leaves fall away in autumn, greenish young cones are visible near the tips of the branches and older brown cones are farther back.

Young Douglas fir cones

Mature cone

THE "FAKE" FIR
True firs have upright cones that fall apart high up on the tree. The unrelated Douglas fir has hanging cones that fall to the ground in one piece.

Cones become hard and brown when mature

SMALL CONES
The western red cedar, a species of thuja (p. 31), has clusters of tiny cones perched among its leaves - quite unlike the cones of true cedars.

A SHORT LIFE
Spruce cones are smooth and slightly flexible, unlike hard pine cones. They fall soon after releasing their seeds.

Young cones on branch

Mature cones

ROUND CONES
Cypress cones are small and rounded, and often grow in clusters. The cones shown here belong to the Lawson cypress, which is often found in gardens. When the cones are young, they are blue-green and tightly closed.

OPENING UP
Cypress cones have 6-12 disklike scales that gradually part from each other as the cone matures. Monterey cypress cones are unusually large, and their scales are visible.

A GIANT'S CONES
The giant sequoia has small, round cones that take two years to ripen.

Disintegrating cone

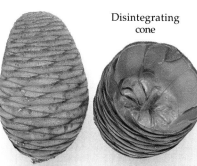

Scale with seeds attached

EGG-SHAPED CONES
The cones of true cedars are smooth and egg-shaped. They consist of a spiral stack of scales, each of which has two seeds attached to it. When a cone is mature, the tip breaks up, and very gradually all the scales fall to the ground.

ON SHOW
Cedar cones sit upright on the branches. They take up to three years to mature and a number of years to disintegrate.

INSIDE A PINE CONE
It takes up to three years for the female pine "flower" to develop into the familiar seed-bearing cone. At first the cone is soft and about the size of a pea but, after pollination, it grows and hardens. During this process it changes color from dark green to brown as most of the cells within it become lignified (made woody). Pine seeds develop in pairs, with two seeds being attached to each scale in the cone. Each seed has a delicate wing, which is pressed against the scale for protection. In the stone pine, whose cone is shown here sliced in half, the seeds are large and have a tough shell. These seeds are the pine kernels that are used in cooking.

Shell surrounding seed kernel

Young cone

Mature cone

Scale

Young green cones

NATIVE PINE
The Scotch pine has small pointed cones. This species is one of only three conifers native to Britain, the others being the yew and the juniper.

Mature cone

Scotch pine seeds

Scales open in dry weather

Scales close completely in wet weather

Scales begin to close when air becomes moister

A CHANGE IN THE WEATHER?
Pine cones are traditionally used to forecast the weather - a piece of country lore that does actually contain a grain of truth. As these cones show, their scales can be open or tightly shut. Cones release their seeds in dry weather; when it is damp, the scales close up to keep the seeds dry.

WHITE TIPS
White, or Weymouth, pine is one of a number of pines that have long, cylindrical cones that look like spruce cones in outline. The white marks at the tips of the scales are spots of resin that oozes from the young cone.

Paired cones of cluster pine

Sugar pine seeds have wings up to 1.5 in (4 cm) long

CONES IN CLUSTERS
Cones develop from female "flowers" that grow in groups on developing shoots. Because the cones may stay on the trees for many years, this can create branches that have clusters of cones at regular intervals along their length. Many pines have cones that develop in pairs.

Old cone that has shed most of its seeds

CALIFORNIAN GIANT
The sugar pine has some of the largest cones of any conifer. The cones are usually about 15 in (40 cm) long, but in some specimens they can reach lengths of nearly 2 ft (60 cm). A single cone can weigh as much as 1.1 lb (500 g). Sugar pines are found in the mountain areas of the western United States. They get their name from the resin they produce, which has a sweet taste unlike that of most pines.

Falling leaves

LEAVES GET THEIR COLOR from the green pigment they contain called chlorophyll, which harnesses the energy in sunlight. To make the most of the sunlight falling on their leaves, plants often have "accessory" pigments as well. These absorb light of different wavelengths and pass the energy on to the chlorophyll. The main accessory pigments are carotenoids, which can be orange, yellow, or red; xanthophylls, which are yellow; and anthocyanins, which are purple, scarlet, and blue. Before a deciduous tree sheds its leaves, the balance of these pigments changes, and the result is often a brilliant burst of color.

CLIMATIC VARIATION
Cherry leaves turn red or yellow, depending on both tree and climate. In some years the colors are much stronger than in others.

BRED FOR COLOR
Some ornamental trees are grown especially for their autumn colors. Maples are well known for their bright autumn tints, and in the exquisite Japanese maples, oriental-plant breeders have attempted to improve on nature by emphasizing this feature.

AMERICAN FALL
The eye-catching colors of a New England autumn are produced mainly by oaks and sugar maples.

GARDEN GLORY
Persian ironwood has some of the richest autumn colors of all trees found in gardens. The reds, oranges, and yellows in its leaves are created by carotenoid and anthocyanin pigments. Carotenoids get their name from the fact that they make carrots orange. They also provide the color of many other vegetables, fruits, and flowers.

Yellow color produced by a carotenoid pigment

DESIGNED FOR DISPOSAL
Each year a deciduous tree like the horse chestnut invests a huge amount of energy in producing new leaves and then throwing them away. One advantage of disposable leaves is that it does not matter too much if they get damaged. Unlike the evergreen conifers, deciduous trees do not need resins or a thick coating of wax to protect their leaves.

COLORFUL RELATIVES
The more sugars that a leaf contains, the brighter its autumn colors are likely to be. The sycamore, a European maple, has fairly bright autumn colors, but they cannot rival the brilliance of American maples. This is because the more extreme American climate helps a tree to produce sugars and, from them, makes more anthocyanins.

WHY LEAVES FALL
As autumn proceeds, a layer of cork grows across the leaf stalk, eventually causing the death of the leaf.

Next year's bud
Leaf stalk
Corky layer

PIGMENT DESTRUCTION
These leaves from a snake-bark maple show how the destruction of chlorophyll, which began at the outer edges of the leaf, is gradually working inward.

TRANSATLANTIC COLOR SPECTRUM
Most European oaks turn a dull brown in autumn, while in North America the leaves of some red oaks turn bright crimson.

Area with chlorophyll
Area without chlorophyll

HOLDING ON
Not all dead leaves are shed immediately. Young beeches keep many of their leaves until the next spring.

WASTE REMOVAL
Like animals, plants must get rid of toxic waste products. As well as reabsorbing minerals from its leaves, a tree also deposits waste products in them before they fall. This produces brownish colors, as in this tulip tree leaf.

INTERNAL DESTRUCTION
In this hickory leaflet, the chlorophyll is being destroyed not only inward from the leaf edge, but also outward from the leaf's midrib.

CHANGING COLOR
As a leaf dies, the carotenoids in it may undergo a series of chemical changes in which they turn from yellow to orange to red. At the same time, scarlet anthocyanins are produced from sugars in the leaf.

The death of a tree

FROM THE MOMENT THEY GERMINATE, trees live side by side with the organisms that will eventually kill them. Insects create small wounds in their wood, ivy scrambles up their trunks, and a deadly rain of fungal spores settles on their branches, ready to infect any point of weakness. Bit by bit, the tree surrenders parts of itself to its attacker, sealing off rotten branches and decaying heartwood in an attempt to stay alive. The battle may be waged for years, but inevitably less and less living wood remains, until one spring the sap no longer rises and the tree is dead.

PETRIFIED WOOD
Most wood soon decays, but if buried in water-logged conditions or in peat it may become petrified wood, in which the wood's shape is preserved by minerals.

Deer feed on the bark of saplings, thereby cutting off their sap supply

COMPETING FOR LIGHT
Ivy weakens trees by reducing the light supply. As ivy climbs up a tree, it uses tiny rootlets to anchor itself onto the trunk and branches. Although the rootlets absorb moisture from the bark, they do not penetrate the wood.

Thick, shiny leaves reduce water loss

DOUBLE TRUNKS
The left of these two trunks is actually the stem of an old ivy plant.

A LIVING CARPET
Once wood rots, it soaks up water like a sponge, making it a perfect surface for moisture-loving plants to grow on. This dead log is covered by ferns and mosses. Like fungi, ferns and mosses grow from spores - tiny cells that are wafted through the air by the breeze.

DUST TO DUST
When wood decays, the minerals that it contains find their way back into the soil to be taken up by living trees. In mature forests, growth and decay are finely balanced.

Adult male stag beetle

Stag beetle larva

ROTTING AWAY
Living wood has many chemical defenses against attack by fungi, but once wood has died, the chemicals gradually break down and are no longer effective. This branch shows the result of five years' decay on a woodland floor.

FEEDING ON WOOD
The larva of the stag beetle feeds on decaying wood. Wood lice feed mainly on fungi, rotting leaves, and other dead plant matter.

Wood lice

Evergreen fronds of polypody fern

THE HIDDEN LIFE OF FUNGI
Fungi may feed on dead or living wood. Toadstools, which are produced by certain types of fungi, appear only when the fungi needs to produce spores. The long slender strands through which fungi feed are hidden from sight inside the wood.

Toadstools growing in dead wood

IN AT THE KILL
Many woodland fungi can continue to live on the remains of a tree after it is dead. These toadstools are sprouting from a decaying stump.

CREEPING DEATH
An attack by honey fungus often spells death for a tree. The fungus spreads by spores and by thick strands, sometimes known as "bootlaces." These grow between a tree's bark and wood.

SPREADING BY SPORES
Fungi spread mainly by their spores. Most toadstools produce spores on gills that hang vertically from the toadstool's cap.

Wood

BRACKET FUNGUS
The many different species of bracket fungus grow on both living and dead wood. Although they are often slow-growing, they probably kill more trees than any other group of fungi. Unlike most gilled toadstools, the brackets are hard and survive for a number of years. Their spores are usually dispersed from round pores.

Underside of bracket showing spore-producing pores

HARMLESS GUESTS
Plants that live on trees are divided into two types. Parasites, like mistletoe, live on nutrients "stolen" from their tree host. Epiphytes, like these tropical bromeliads, just use a tree as a perch and do it no harm.

INSIDE ATTACK
The larvae of longhorn beetles damage trees by chewing through the living wood.

Moss

Life among the leaves

M OST OF THE ANIMALS that live on trees are invertebrates, or animals without backbones. Every tree is home to vast numbers of microscopic nematode worms, and also to thousands or even millions of insects. For example, nearly 300 species of insects live on mature oak trees; more than a hundred are moths whose caterpillars live on or even in oak leaves. To combat this drain on their resources, trees use chemical weapons in their leaves and wood, and many produce a second flush of leaves in midsummer. This makes up for the losses that they suffer in spring.

FEASTING ON LEAVES
Many leaves are eaten by insect larvae. Some, like these beetle larvae, feed just on the cells between the leaf veins.

Adult gall wasp

Gall falls from leaf in late summer; larva develops in leaf litter

Oak apple gall

Oak marble gall

LEAF GALLS
Galls develop on leaves as well as on stems. Button-shaped oak spangle galls each contain a single larva of a wasp; bean galls on willow leaves are caused by the larva of a sawfly.

Spangle galls on oak leaf

Bean galls on willow leaves

GALLS AND GROWTHS
Galls (swellings) are created when a tree reacts to an intruder - often the larva of a tiny wasp. The larva turns this abnormal growth to its advantage by living and feeding within the protective layer formed by the gall.

LEAF INSECTS
These remarkable tropical insects are perfectly camouflaged to look like the leaves they live among.

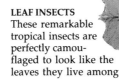

TREETOP PREDATOR
The pine marten is one of the few predatory mammals that lives among the treetops. It feeds at night on roosting birds, eggs, insects, and fruit.

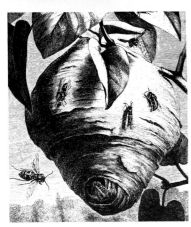

Wasp nest hanging from tree

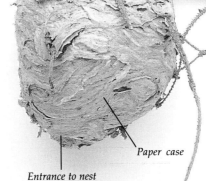

Paper case

Entrance to nest

THE PAPER NEST
In spring, a queen wasp starts on the task of nest building. She chews wood fibers and mixes them with saliva, shaping the pulp into shell-like layers of paper which she hangs from a branch or hole in a tree. After her first batch of eggs hatch, the queen takes no part in further nest-building. The young wasps carry on the task and also collect food for the queen, who spends all her time laying more eggs to increase the size of the colony.

Pine beauty moth

Purple emperor

White admiral

Oak eggar moth

BUTTERFLIES AND MOTHS

The caterpillars of woodland butterflies and moths feed on the leaves of trees or ground plants such as violets and bramble. Although most do little damage, the pine beauty moth is a serious pest in conifer plantations.

WINTER QUARTERS

Every autumn, monarch butterflies migrate southward to Mexico, where they spend the winter crowded together on pine tree trunks. All the monarchs in North America fly to the same few pine woods every year.

FUNGUS ATTACK

Leaves are often attacked by fungi. These sycamore leaves have been attacked by tar spot fungus - a sign that the tree grew in unpolluted air.

Infected patches turn black and expand

More and more patches of fungus appear during the summer; over half the leaf may be covered by the time it falls in autumn

Acorns attacked by weevils

Hazelnuts eaten by voles

Weevil

FEEDING ON SEEDS

Seeds and nuts are attacked both on the tree and on the ground. Weevils are specialist seed-eaters; some bore holes in acorns with the aid of their long, probing "snouts."

HOME AMONG THE BRANCHES

The tangled lower branches of small trees provide cover for the nests of birds like the chaffinch. This finch makes its nests from moss, lichen, and hair.

Chaffinch

Cherry leaf eaten by caterpillar

Insect pupa attached to oak leaf

Cherry leaf mined by micromoth caterpillar

INSECT ONSLAUGHT

The caterpillars of micromoths are so small that they can squeeze between the upper and lower surfaces of leaves, tunneling as they feed.

Leaf-eating mammals

The only large mammals to live and feed on trees are found in the tropics, where trees are in leaf all year. Leaves are somewhat hard to digest, so the animals spend much of the day eating to get enough nourishment.

THREE-TOED SLOTH

This bizarre South American animal spends most of its life hanging upside down.

KOALA BEAR

Koalas live almost entirely on eucalyptus leaves (p. 13).

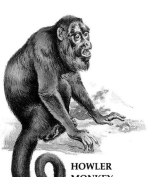

HOWLER MONKEY

Slow-moving South American howler monkeys use their tails as a fifth limb. This helps them to climb through the treetops in search of leaves.

Life in the leaf litter

Every autumn a mature oak tree may shed something like a quarter of a million leaves. Why then doesn't the ground beneath trees become piled high with leaves as one autumn follows another? The answer is that once on the ground, leaves break down and decay. When a leaf falls, it becomes part of the leaf litter - the top layer of ground that is made up of whole leaves and leaf fragments. As the leaf is buried by other leaves, bacteria and fungi feed on it, causing it to decay. Finally, all that remains of the leaf is a crumbly substance called humus. This provides nutrients for growing plants, and so the substances in falling leaves are continually recycled.

Magnolia leaf skeletons

LEAF SKELETONS
Sometimes the leaf rots a little and then dries out before the tougher veins and midrib begin to decompose. This produces a leaf skeleton.

HIDING AMONG THE LEAVES
Toads often hibernate under logs surrounded by leaves and leaf litter. Although they are not true woodland animals, they find plenty to eat on the woodland floor before they enter hibernation. In North America many kinds of salamanders, which are also amphibians, use damp leaves as a refuge in the heat of summer.

MIXED LEAF LITTER
This litter is from a mixed deciduous forest, and contains oak, maple, and beech leaves. The rate at which the leaves of different species rot varies. The leaves of maples, for example, rot quite quickly. Damp conditions will speed up the rotting process.

BEECH LITTER
Beech leaves rot very slowly. When they do eventually decay, they produce more acid humus than that in a mixed forest.

THE END PRODUCT
The black specks seen here are humus - tree remains that have been completely broken down.

Germinating ash seeds

GERMINATING SEEDS
As leaves break down, the minerals they contain are released. These minerals can then be absorbed by other plants, including trees themselves.

Millipede

Centipede

Pill millipedes

Springtail a wingless insect

Pseudoscorpion

A HIDDEN WORLD
Scavengers like pseudoscorpions and the animals that feed on them live in leaf litter.

Thuidium tamariscinum, a moss

HORIZONTAL GROWTH
The wood anemone spreads through the humus with underground stems. On gray days, its delicate flowers droop and close up for protection from rain.

MOISTURE LOVERS
Mosses are small, flowerless plants that reproduce by releasing millions of tiny spores. Many mosses live in damp woodlands.

EARLY INTO FLOWER
In deciduous forests, small plants such as primroses flower before the tree leaves open, when plenty of light still reaches the ground.

LIVERWORTS
These simple plants do not produce flowers. They are common in damp woodland on the banks of streams.

Winged ant

WOODLAND BUILDERS
In deciduous forests, most species of ant nest under logs and tree stumps; in coniferous forests, wood ants build high mounds of pine needles.

Nest of wood ant

BANDED SNAILS
The patterns and colors of these snail shells are for camouflage.

The coniferous forest floor

The scales and needles of conifers take longer to decompose than the leaves of broadleaved trees, and the humus they produce is quite acid. Together with the year-round shade in thick coniferous forests, the acid leaf litter prevents many plants from establishing themselves. Where gaps between the trees let in light, acid-tolerant plants such as ferns spring up. Fungi thrive in coniferous leaf litter and produce large numbers of toadstools in the autumn.

Fern fronds unrolling in spring

Forest floor fungi

Cones gnawed by squirrels

Ground beetles

Pine leaf litter

Bilberry in flower

53

Pollution and disease

THE COMPLICATED PROCESSES that power a tree's growth need clean air if they are to work efficiently. Across many parts of the world, the air is now highly polluted by fumes from cars, and gases from factories and power stations. These fumes reach high into the atmosphere and mix with water and other chemicals to form rain that can be as acid as vinegar. Although there is much argument about the processes involved, there is little doubt that this "acid rain" is responsible for the decline of many forests.

A DYING FOREST
Acid rain damage was first noticed in the early 1970s, largely through its disastrous effect on the wildlife of Scandinavian lakes. Since then it has hit coniferous forests throughout central Europe, especially in Germany and Switzerland. It is also an increasing problem in North America, particularly in the industrialized northeast United States and in eastern Canada.

HEALTHY TREE
The damage caused by pollution such as acid rain strikes both coniferous and broadleaved trees. It is easiest to see in conifers, such as the yew, because conifer scales and needles normally stay on the tree for a number of years. As a result, any signs of sickness have a chance to build up.

A FUTURE IN DOUBT
Churchyard yew trees are often centuries old. Acid rain caused by air pollution may now threaten their survival.

Long shoots indicate healthy growth

Discoloration of leaves - this may be a direct effect of acid rain, which enables ozone in the atmosphere to disrupt the chemistry of the leaves

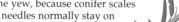

Deep green color shows that the leaf is full of chlorophyll, the substance which is essential in harnessing the sun's energy (pp. 26 and 46)

Healthy leaves survive well back on each twig and along the branches

CITY DWELLER
The London plane fares better in polluted urban air than many other trees. Whereas most city trees become blackened with grime, it sheds the outermost layers of its bark in large patches, revealing cream-colored young bark underneath.

54

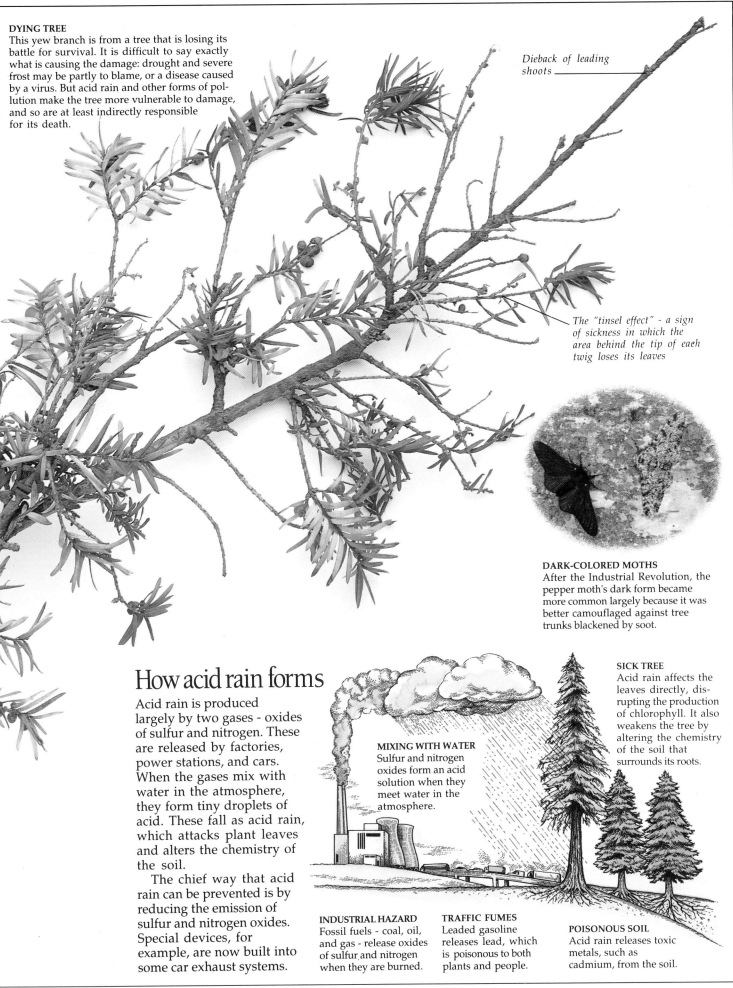

DYING TREE

This yew branch is from a tree that is losing its battle for survival. It is difficult to say exactly what is causing the damage: drought and severe frost may be partly to blame, or a disease caused by a virus. But acid rain and other forms of pollution make the tree more vulnerable to damage, and so are at least indirectly responsible for its death.

Dieback of leading shoots

The "tinsel effect" - a sign of sickness in which the area behind the tip of each twig loses its leaves

DARK-COLORED MOTHS

After the Industrial Revolution, the pepper moth's dark form became more common largely because it was better camouflaged against tree trunks blackened by soot.

How acid rain forms

Acid rain is produced largely by two gases - oxides of sulfur and nitrogen. These are released by factories, power stations, and cars. When the gases mix with water in the atmosphere, they form tiny droplets of acid. These fall as acid rain, which attacks plant leaves and alters the chemistry of the soil.

The chief way that acid rain can be prevented is by reducing the emission of sulfur and nitrogen oxides. Special devices, for example, are now built into some car exhaust systems.

MIXING WITH WATER
Sulfur and nitrogen oxides form an acid solution when they meet water in the atmosphere.

SICK TREE
Acid rain affects the leaves directly, disrupting the production of chlorophyll. It also weakens the tree by altering the chemistry of the soil that surrounds its roots.

INDUSTRIAL HAZARD
Fossil fuels - coal, oil, and gas - release oxides of sulfur and nitrogen when they are burned.

TRAFFIC FUMES
Leaded gasoline releases lead, which is poisonous to both plants and people.

POISONOUS SOIL
Acid rain releases toxic metals, such as cadmium, from the soil.

From tree to timber

BEFORE THE ARRIVAL of steam-powered and then gasoline-powered engines, turning trees into timber required a great deal of labor. Felling a tree using axes was the easy part; the log then had to be sawed by hand, a process that took many days. Today, almost all the work is done by machines. Power saws make short work of the thickest trunks, and then giant, hydraulically operated jaws handle them on their way to the sawmill. Once at the mill, a log is loaded onto a sliding cradle and is sliced into boards by a giant band saw. The way that a log is sawed depends on the type of timber and what it will be used for. Two simple methods of cutting are shown here; many other methods, like sawing "in the round," produce a complex pattern of boards and smaller timber. All these methods are designed to get the greatest amount of good quality wood from a log. Nothing is wasted: whatever is left over will end up as chipboard or pulp.

THE SPRING LOG RUN
Water power was the traditional way to get logs to the sawmill in North America. Breaking up log jams was a skilled business that called for perfect balance. Log runs like the one shown here caused great environmental damage to the water and the banks of rivers; today they are rarely seen.

FOREST SAWMILL
As settlers moved farther and farther westward in North America, logging camps and sawmills were set up to provide timber for their houses, barns, and wagons.

"THROUGH AND THROUGH" SAWING
This is the simplest way of sawing a log. However, the way the cuts are made through the grain means that the boards that it produces are liable to warp, so it is rarely used with expensive timber.

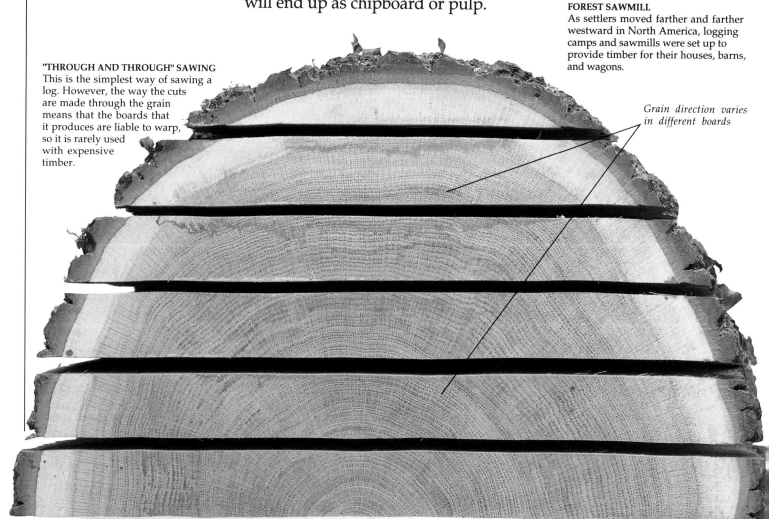

Grain direction varies in different boards

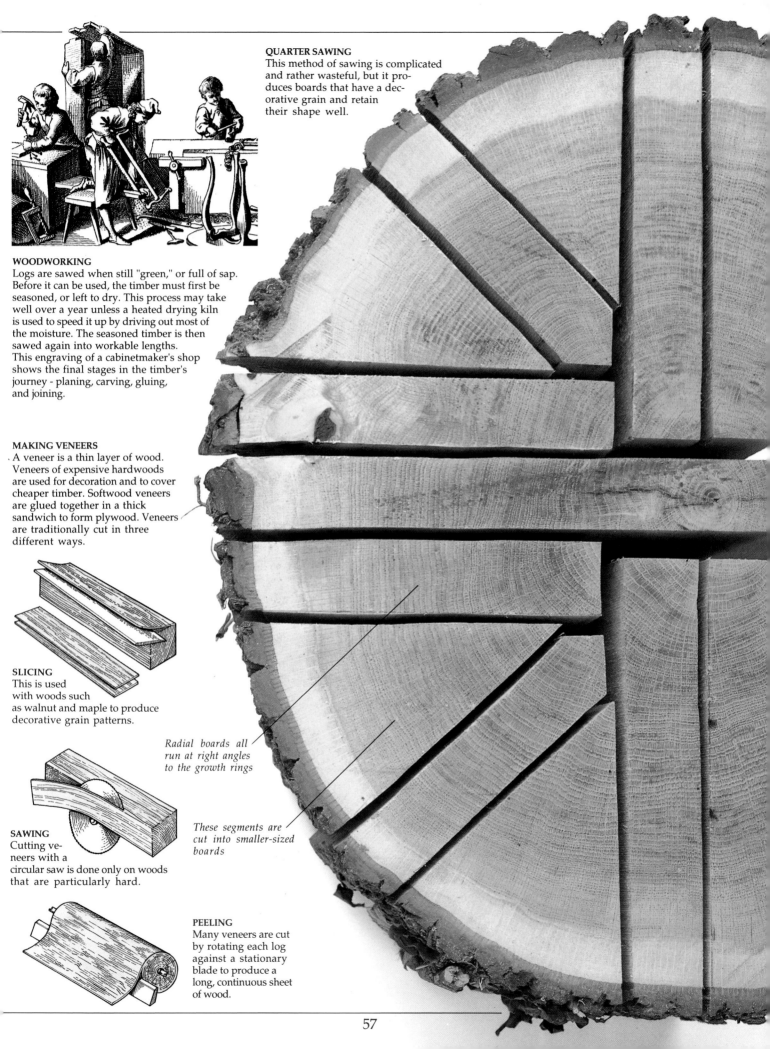

QUARTER SAWING
This method of sawing is complicated and rather wasteful, but it produces boards that have a decorative grain and retain their shape well.

WOODWORKING
Logs are sawed when still "green," or full of sap. Before it can be used, the timber must first be seasoned, or left to dry. This process may take well over a year unless a heated drying kiln is used to speed it up by driving out most of the moisture. The seasoned timber is then sawed again into workable lengths. This engraving of a cabinetmaker's shop shows the final stages in the timber's journey - planing, carving, gluing, and joining.

MAKING VENEERS
A veneer is a thin layer of wood. Veneers of expensive hardwoods are used for decoration and to cover cheaper timber. Softwood veneers are glued together in a thick sandwich to form plywood. Veneers are traditionally cut in three different ways.

SLICING
This is used with woods such as walnut and maple to produce decorative grain patterns.

SAWING
Cutting veneers with a circular saw is done only on woods that are particularly hard.

PEELING
Many veneers are cut by rotating each log against a stationary blade to produce a long, continuous sheet of wood.

Radial boards all run at right angles to the growth rings

These segments are cut into smaller-sized boards

Working with wood

PEOPLE WHO WORK WITH WOOD traditionally divide it into two types - "hardwood," which comes from broadleaved trees, and "softwood," which comes from conifers. Sometimes these two words can be misleading. Yew, for example, is a softwood, but it is actually as hard as oak. Balsa, on the other hand, is a hardwood. The hundreds of different types of timber produced by the world's trees vary enormously. The heaviest wood, grown by an African tree related to the olive, is so dense that it sinks like a stone in water. At the other end of the scale, balsa is so light that a four-inch (ten-centimeter) cube of it can weigh as little as 1.5 oz (40 g).

Melanesian wood carving

Light pinkish coloring typical of freshly cut cherry wood

Planed cherry wood

Knot

Planed yew

Close grain produced by slow growth

Unplaned yew

Dense knots typical of yew wood

CHANGING COLOR
Many woods change color when they are exposed to the air. Freshly cut cherry wood is light with just a tinge of pink. As time goes by, cherry wood grows darker, until, in very old pieces of furniture, it becomes a deep red.

THE GUNSMITH'S WOOD
The rich color and swirling grain of polished walnut makes it one of the cabinetmaker's most prized materials. It is also traditionally used to make the stocks of guns: walnut can be worked into a comfortable shape, and it can stand, without splitting, the jolt of a gun being fired.

THE BOW MAKER'S WOOD
Yew grows very slowly, and this gives the wood great weight and strength. Thin, springy yew branches were once used for making longbows. Today, wood from yew trunks is often cut in thin layers and used as a decorative veneer.

THE MERRY MAYPOLE
Dancing around a wooden pole is a custom that dates back to pagan times. The pole has been made from a variety of different woods.

THE VERSATILE LARCH
Wherever a cheap, tough wood is needed, larch is often the ideal choice. The best quality wood is used in furniture making and boat building; much of the rest ends up as pulp that is used in the manufacture of paper.

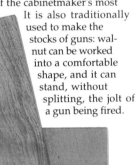

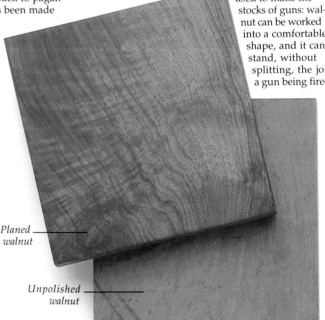

Planed walnut

Unpolished walnut

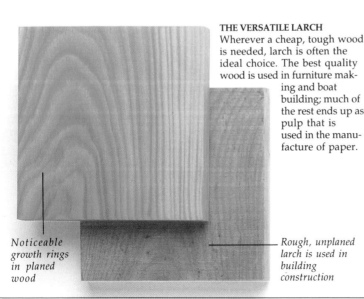

Noticeable growth rings in planed wood

Rough, unplaned larch is used in building construction

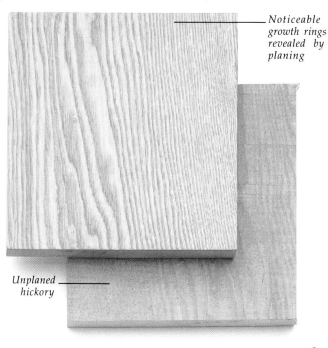

Noticeable growth rings revealed by planing

Unplaned hickory

Grain "interlocked," or banded in alternating directions - a common feature in tropical timbers

Unplaned wood showing color produced by prolonged exposure to air

NATURE'S SHOCK ABSORBER

It takes a very heavy blow to shatter a piece of ash wood, and this makes ash ideal for the handles of axes and spades. In Europe, ash wood was always the first choice for the handles of tools until hickory started to be exported from North America. Hickory is an even better shock absorber than ash.

SKILLED WOODWORKER

This engraving is one of a series that depicts different skills. It shows a turner, a craftsman who makes "turned" wooden objects using a lathe. The craft dates back to the ancient Egyptians, who made many turned chair legs and stools of surprising quality.

TROPICAL TREASURE

Mahogany became highly prized after Spanish sailors brought back a gift of Caribbean mahogany for King Philip II in the 16th century. Since then, 400 years of reckless felling have all but exhausted the stock of wild mahogany, and with it, much of the world's best hardwood forests.

Planed iroko

Natural chemicals protect iroko from attack by fungi

Unplaned iroko

Planed oak

Sap-conducting pores appear as tiny streaks in the grain of oak

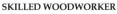

Unplaned oak

WITHSTANDING THE ELEMENTS

Woods vary in the way they stand up to rain and decay. A garden bench made of beech would collapse within a few years, while one made of the tropical timber iroko would last for decades. Iroko is often used as a substitute for teak.

HEART OF OAK

Oak is one of the strongest and most durable timbers in the world. Huge beams of oak were once used in building. To support the dome of St. Paul's Cathedral in London, for example, Sir Christopher Wren ordered oak beams nearly 50 ft (15 m) long.

Tree care and management

Natural woodlands have been "managed" by people since prehistoric times, chiefly by special techniques such as coppicing (regularly cutting trees at ground level), pollarding (lopping the tops of trees), and selective felling of trees so that various kinds of timber can be produced as a renewable crop. Tree planting probably began with species like the olive and date palm (pp. 39 and 43), which were grown for their fruit. In the wild, trees often become damaged or distorted by overcrowding, disease, and exposure to wind and rain, so tree cultivation also involves keeping them healthy and vigorous. Thinning out trees reduces the competition for light and nutrients, so that those that are left grow better. Pruning and grafting help to shape a tree, prevent disease, and increase fruit yields.

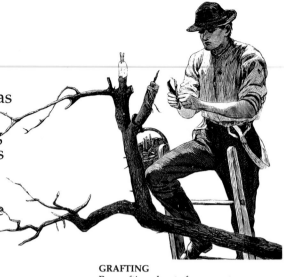

GRAFTING
By grafting shoots from one tree on to the branches or trunk of another, it is possible to introduce good characteristics, such as healthy fruit or a strong trunk.

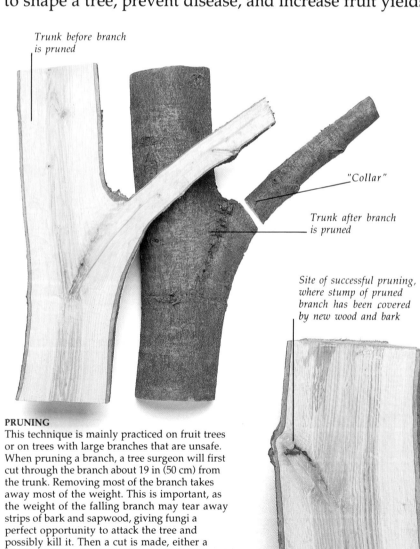

Trunk before branch is pruned

"Collar"

Trunk after branch is pruned

Site of successful pruning, where stump of pruned branch has been covered by new wood and bark

Hole left by wood rotting after branch has fallen away, leaving damp wood vulnerable to attack by fungi

PRUNING
This technique is mainly practiced on fruit trees or on trees with large branches that are unsafe. When pruning a branch, a tree surgeon will first cut through the branch about 19 in (50 cm) from the trunk. Removing most of the branch takes away most of the weight. This is important, as the weight of the falling branch may tear away strips of bark and sapwood, giving fungi a perfect opportunity to attack the tree and possibly kill it. Then a cut is made, either a "flush cut," close to the trunk, or sometimes a cut at the "collar," the point where the branch begins to widen just before meeting the trunk. The exposed wood is then treated with a waterproofing agent and a fungicide. As the tree grows, the wood will become covered with a layer of living wood and protective bark.

WATER TRAPS
Where branches have broken off and not healed, holes can be left that hold pools of water. The decayed wood has to be scraped out before the hole is treated and blocked. Likewise, where branches meet to form natural cups, water may collect and provoke fungal attack. This type of water trap can be dealt with by cutting a drainage channel through the wood, or by permanently inserting a metal tube which drains off the water.

Coppicing and pollarding

Coppiced trees are regularly cut at ground level so that they produce a cluster of straight stems which can be harvested and used as poles or for fencing. Pollarded trees regularly have their tops cut off; these produce long, straight branches from shoots that are too high to be damaged by cattle and deer.

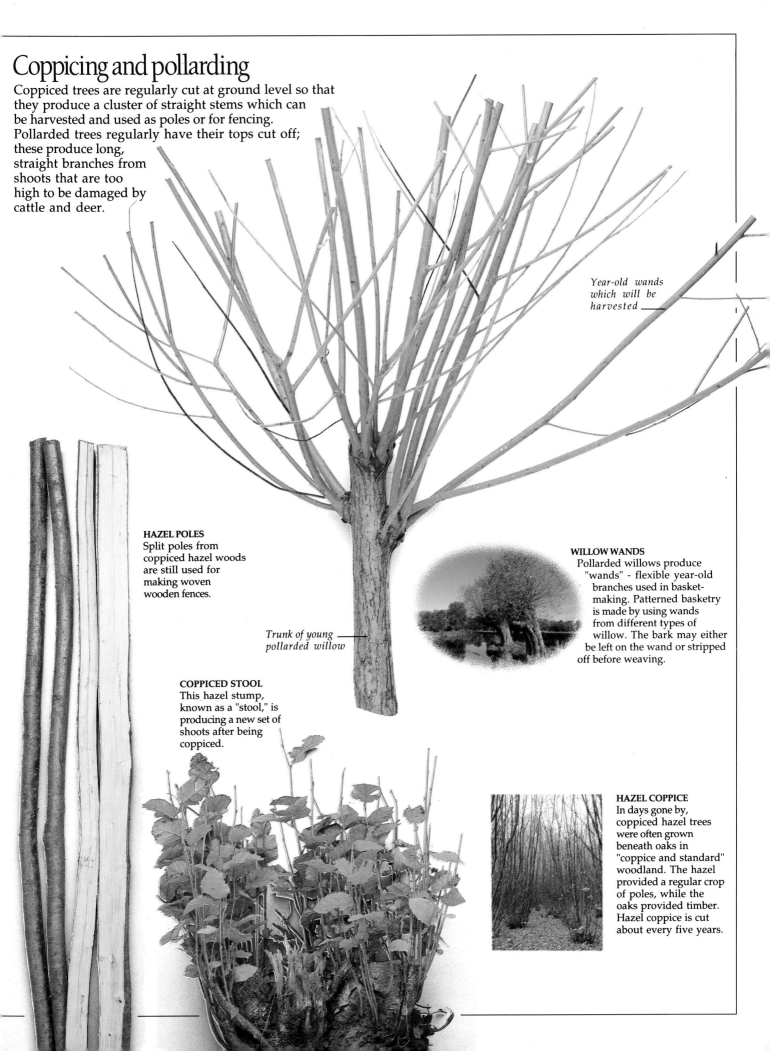

Year-old wands which will be harvested

HAZEL POLES
Split poles from coppiced hazel woods are still used for making woven wooden fences.

Trunk of young pollarded willow

COPPICED STOOL
This hazel stump, known as a "stool," is producing a new set of shoots after being coppiced.

WILLOW WANDS
Pollarded willows produce "wands" - flexible year-old branches used in basket-making. Patterned basketry is made by using wands from different types of willow. The bark may either be left on the wand or stripped off before weaving.

HAZEL COPPICE
In days gone by, coppiced hazel trees were often grown beneath oaks in "coppice and standard" woodland. The hazel provided a regular crop of poles, while the oaks provided timber. Hazel coppice is cut about every five years.

Botanist Sir Joseph Dalton Hooker (1817-1911) collecting trees and plants in the Himalayas

Looking at trees

FOR ANYONE INTERESTED IN PRACTICAL NATURAL HISTORY, studying trees can be a fascinating year-round hobby. Trees have two useful characteristics; unlike animals, they don't move around, and unlike most other plants, they don't die back in the winter. As a result, it is easy to follow the progress of the same trees throughout the year. Because many different parts of trees can be dried and stored almost indefinitely, it is easy to build up a collection that will help you to identify different species and understand how they grow.

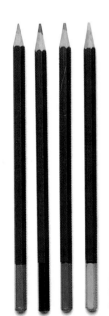

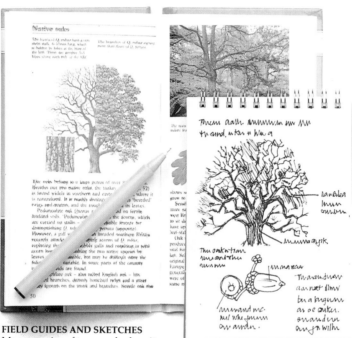

Unbreakable lens for use outdoors

Large magnifying glass for indoor use

TREES IN CLOSE-UP
A magnifying glass will enable you to see structures like the different parts of wind-pollinated flowers and the tiny seeds of trees such as the birches.

A selection of colored crayons is useful for making tree "portraits"

FIELD GUIDES AND SKETCHES
Many species of tree can look quite similar. A good field guide will help you to tell them apart and provide interesting information. Drawing, however, is probably the best way of learning the distinctive shapes of different trees.

TAKING PHOTOGRAPHS
One of the most interesting ways to photograph trees is to take pictures of the same tree in all the seasons of the year.

Plastic bags are good for collecting, but paper bags, which allow moisture to escape, are better for storing

Large plastic bags for collecting leaves, leaf-litter, and seeds

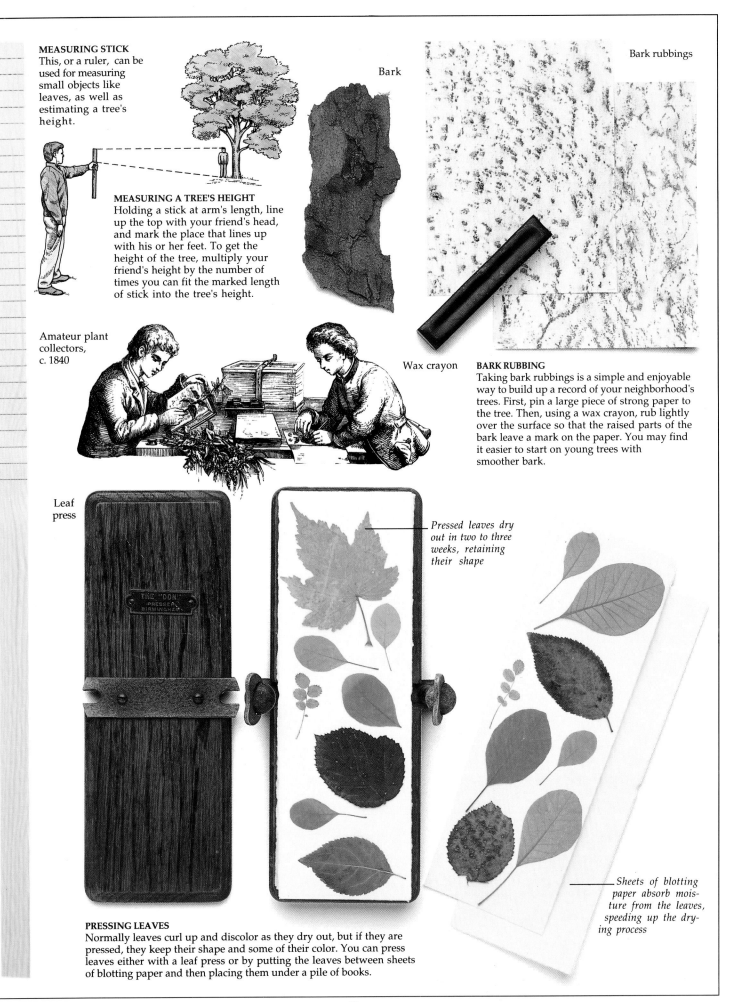

MEASURING STICK
This, or a ruler, can be used for measuring small objects like leaves, as well as estimating a tree's height.

MEASURING A TREE'S HEIGHT
Holding a stick at arm's length, line up the top with your friend's head, and mark the place that lines up with his or her feet. To get the height of the tree, multiply your friend's height by the number of times you can fit the marked length of stick into the tree's height.

Bark

Bark rubbings

Amateur plant collectors, c. 1840

Wax crayon

BARK RUBBING
Taking bark rubbings is a simple and enjoyable way to build up a record of your neighborhood's trees. First, pin a large piece of strong paper to the tree. Then, using a wax crayon, rub lightly over the surface so that the raised parts of the bark leave a mark on the paper. You may find it easier to start on young trees with smoother bark.

Leaf press

Pressed leaves dry out in two to three weeks, retaining their shape

Sheets of blotting paper absorb moisture from the leaves, speeding up the drying process

PRESSING LEAVES
Normally leaves curl up and discolor as they dry out, but if they are pressed, they keep their shape and some of their color. You can press leaves either with a leaf press or by putting the leaves between sheets of blotting paper and then placing them under a pile of books.

Index

Acknowledgments

The author and Dorling Kindersley would like to thank: the curator and staff, Westonbird Arboretum; Simon White of the Botanic Gardens, Bath; Linda Gamlin; George Wiltshire; Forestry Commission, Alice Holt Lodge; and Marika Rae for their advice and help in supplying specimens for photography.
Mark Ricks Tree Services of Bath for supplying and transporting the large specimens.
Ken Day for supplying sawn sections and prepared timbers.
Arthur Chater, Caroline Whiteford, Gary Summons and Chris Owen at the Natural History Museum.
Ray Owen for artwork.
Gabrielle Bamford for typing.

Picture credits
t=top b=bottom m=middle l=left r=right

Heather Angel: 18b; 61b
BPCC/Aldus Archive: 7b; 12ml, r; 22t; 45t
Chris Beetles Ltd: 10m
G I Bernard/Oxford Scientific Films: 24mr
Bridgeman Art Library/Bonhams: 6bl
Dr Jeremy Burgess/Science Photo Library: 32b
Jane Burton/Bruce Coleman Ltd: 24ml
Robert Burton/Bruce Coleman Ltd: 48m
Jim Clare/Partridge Films Ltd/OSF: 20ml, mr
Eric Crichton/Bruce Coleman Ltd: 32m; 36m
Stephen Dalton/NHPA: 21mb
J Deane/Bruce Coleman Ltd: 21t
Mansell Collection: 19b; 41b; 53t
Mary Evans Picture Library: 6br; 12t;

23t; 37m; 38t; 43mr; 51m, br; 56tl; 57t; 59; 60t; 62t
Fine Art Photographic Library: 8m; 11b
Jeff Foott/Bruce Coleman Ltd : 51t
John Freeman: 56tr
Linda Gamlin: 16tl
David Grewcock/Frank Lane: 48tr
Brian Hawkes/NHPA: 16b
Michael Holford: 6t; 58t
Eric and David Hosking: 16mr; 21tm
E A James/NHPA: 9mr
J Koivula/Science Source: 23m
Frank Lane: 16ml; 50ml
R P Lawrence/Frank Lane: 24b
Laura Lushington/Sonia Halliday Photographs: 42r
John Mason/Ardea: 49m
G A Mather/Robert Harding: 16tr
G J H Moon/Frank Lane: 9ml
M Newman/Frank Lane: 48tl
Fritz Prensel/Bruce Coleman Ltd: 13t
Hans Reinhard/Bruce Coleman Ltd: 19m; 21b; 50mr
Silvestris/Frank Lane: 54

Kim Taylor/Bruce Coleman Ltd: 53b; 55
Roger Tidman/Frank Lane: 61m
Roger Tidman/NHPA: 14
Norman Tomalin/Bruce Coleman Ltd: 18m
L West/Frank Lane: 46
Christian Zuber/Bruce Coleman Ltd: 42ml

Illustrations by: Coral Mula; Mick Loates and David More of Linden Artists

Picture research by: Millie Trowbridge